MW00936765

Copyright © 2018 by Faith M. Phillips

All rights reserved.

Printed in the United States of America.

No part of this book may be used or reproduced in
any manner whatsoever without written permission,
except in the case of brief quotations embodied in
critical articles and reviews.
For more information, contact the author at
*ReadBooksBy.Faith*

Author's website content designed and maintained
by Geoff Wilson Web Design, Norman, Ok.

Original *Now I Lay Me Down* book cover design by
Kalyn Fay Barnoski.

**Original song lyrics published by permission:**

Carter Sampson, *The Queen of Oklahoma*

Lauren Barth, *While I'm Young*

Kalyn Fay Barnoski, *Bible Belt*

Wink Burcham, *Town In Oklahoma*

Samantha Crain, *Killer*

John Moreland, *Hang Me In The Tulsa County
Stars*

Evan Felker, *The Housefire*

Buffalo Rogers, *Caesar the Crow*

Nellie Clay, *Oklahoma*

John Calvin Abney, *Elastic Highway*

Tequila Kim Reynolds, *About Time*

John Fullbright and Evan Felker, *Pay No Rent*

Carter Sampson, *Wild Bird*

"The note of hope is the only note that can help us from falling to the bottom of the heap of evolution, because, largely, about all a human being is, anyway, is just a hoping machine."

~Woody Guthrie, Pastures of Plenty

# CHAPTER 1

# The Prosecutor

*If I was the Queen of Oklahoma*
*Yes, I could ride the wind.*
~The Queen of Oklahoma, Carter Sampson

The prosecutor stood in the road. She surveyed the scene and said not a word. A denim blouse hung loose on her slender frame. She stared at the ditch, one hand shoved deep in her back pocket. She remembered.

This particular stretch of County Line Road had once been an obscure place in an obscure county, familiar only to the few locals who made their homes on the back road. Obscurity is just another way of saying concealed and the town of Weleetka meets that definition. Interstate 40 runs just a few miles north as the crow flies, ferrying interlopers past long-forgotten Oklahoma towns. It is very much concealed and out of view from the interstate, hidden by stands of trees in rural Okfuskee County. An outsider would never expect to find a town in this pastoral location. Out of sight, out of mind.

The quiet lane that runs through Okfuskee County's back country is populated by trees and an occasional family home. The lawns often hold collections of defunct automobiles and plastic toys left out to fade in the weather. Maxey Parker Reilly hadn't been sure she could find her way back again without some sort of navigation. It had been such a long time since she visited last. She careened her S.U.V. along the blacktop and slowed at each turnoff, eyeing the road signs. But when she came to County Line Road the physical reaction was instant. Total recall took hold and she cut a sharp right. She didn't need to look for signs now. She remembered.

The topography along the road was flat and tree-lined, strewn with thick underbrush. Stationary oil wells provided a gaudy juxtaposition to the otherwise quiet countryside. After a couple of miles hints of color appeared in the ditch like a mirage. Glints of sunlight reflected from multiple points of glass and metal. At first glance it appeared as though flowers had managed to spring up and out of the drab undergrowth. But then a fraction of light angled down from a tree limb, and a plastic whirligig spun in the wind. Then came the teddy bears at the heart of the place, long worn by exposure. Wind chimes played a hollow tune and a light bulb hung from a tree.

The dusty white crosses evidenced a roadside memorial. They are a familiar sight along Oklahoma's highways; a family's way of marking the mournful spot where a loved one drew their final breath in a violent clash of glass and steel. But this roadside memorial was atypical. Small details indicated something very different from a car crash. An American Girl doll with long dark hair and platform heels lay smiling in the dirt. It was the first hint that something might have happened to a little girl here. In the midst of all the odd memorial objects an angel arose. She stood, once gleaming white, now covered in layers of dust thrown up by passing vehicles.

The statue as it stood that day was four feet in height; an elegant effigy with shoulders proud and tall; folds in the long ceramic robe revealed a bent knee. The delicate wingtips of the angel nearly touched the ground. At her bare feet a ceramic puppy and a smiling bear sat on guard next to a basketful of plastic lilies and sparkling beads. The angel cradled a great bouquet of field daisies across her chest. The statue's presence represented a statement to onlookers. Someone had cherished the person who was lost in this place. The angel was carefully chosen to memorialize a child. It was meant to solemnize and express community grief. They placed her at the center of all the other tokens of loss left behind.

But then someone came along, pointed a shotgun at the angel's head and blasted it clean away. It was not the first time the memorial had been violated. Maxey was infuriated by the very sight of it.  Snapshots flashed in her mind from a hot summer evening ten years previous. She had been called out to this place on County Line Road to work one of her very first jobs as the new Okfuskee County Assistant District Attorney. Fresh out of law school, she was eager to prove herself worthy of the position. She often imagined what it would be like to take on a big case. But the pretty young woman was afforded no chance to ease herself into the prosecutor's role. She had been thrown into the deep end by the cold-blooded execution of two little girls on County Line Road, just a few miles outside of Weleetka, and she had no other choice but to swim.

A late model Cavalier approached at a creeping pace and Maxey was at once ready to move. She had seen and remembered enough for one day. The sedan continued to slow as it approached and for a moment her hand moved to her pistol. But the car moved on past. Many years had gone by since the events of that summer in 2008, since the night she received the call that there had been a double murder in Okfuskee County. Now her own children were fast approaching the ages that the two little girls had been when they were gunned down. She knew it was time to tell her unlikely story.

The youngest in a family of all girls, save her doting father, Maxey Parker enjoyed more than her fair share of freedom as a child. Her mother, a talented painter and the local beauty queen by all accounts, took a very liberal approach to parenting. Maxey received some mothering from her older sisters on occasion, but in large part she was left to her own devices. She made her own way and her own rules out of necessity. The independent streak that developed out of caring for herself at such a young age created issues at the school in small town Atoka, Oklahoma. Naturally outspoken, with a brazen streak, Maxey had little motivation for school work. She was much more inclined to cut up in class. She was aware that some of her classmates regarded her as trash because of her wild ways and impudent manner. The teachers scolded and disciplined her on a regular basis. But since she was in effect making her own way, she found no particular sanctity in adulthood. Neither did she feel bound by the rules. She felt joy in defiance. Joy that is, until the day an English teacher introduced her to mock trial.

Maxey took on the State Mock Trial Competition with the same flippant attitude she felt toward school work in general. But this time she crossed an educator who refused to accept less than excellence from an obviously gifted mind. Her twelfth grade teacher, Mrs. Graham, scolded her in front of her peers, not in an attempt to humiliate, but intent on challenging the girl. Mrs. Graham recognized something special in this particular student. She knew it would take a bit more effort than usual to convince her pupil of the same. Maxey revolted at the suggestion to join the mock trial team for weeks until finally her teacher explained in a very stern manner that Maxey was capable of much more than any effort she had put forth thus far. She said that in a class full of hard working students, Maxey did nothing. She demanded to see the full extent of her abilities the next day in the mock trial. Mrs. Graham continued until Maxey Parker, the smart aleck rule breaker, stormed out of the class room crying.

Embarrassed, Maxey went home and for the first time, gave herself an earnest evaluation. She was aware of the trap falls inherent in the life of a poor young Okie girl. Her options would always be limited in her home town. She could either work hard and get out or she could continue to slack, destined to be the small town beauty queen, just like her mother. The latter option was not really an option at all in her mind, so she went to work that night. The salty blonde who loved nothing better than to be out in the wild countryside with a shotgun or a fishing pole, sat down on her bed and began to prepare diligently for mock trial. When she arrived at school the next day she had transformed. She was assigned the role of lead attorney and by the end of the competition she was awarded the 'Best Lawyer' designation.

She had found her purpose in that culmination of preparedness and confidence in a courtroom setting. The girl was locked in. The aptitude she wielded in class didn't just amaze her teacher -- even her classmates were shocked. The class clown had emerged as the master of the mock trial. She understood then where her strengths lay and she began to prepare for the future. One thing she knew for sure, by God, was that she had to get out of Atoka. She set her sights on law school and refused to fall back into a lifestyle that might limit her potential, although she did continue to go fishing from time to time.

Maxey entered the University of Oklahoma College of Law in 2001. She was a bit of a rube with no previous experience in the law profession, save those mock trial victories in high school. Law school social constructs can be a challenge to negotiate. Competitive cults of personality abound in both the student body and among the professors. Upon admission the mass of students are cordoned off into separate sections. In one section you may find the son of a state senator. In most sections you will find at least a handful of fourth generation attorneys. Each section has a military person of some sort in its ranks and a couple of law enforcement veterans, ready to transition from enforcing the law to interpreting it. Passionate idealists pepper the crowd, hungry to dissect the constitution in all its flawed genius, and of course one cannot discount the ambulance chasers. Ambition is the one commonality among the student body, whether it is the ambition to gather dollars, the ambition to achieve political status or ambition to master the labyrinth of the law. Each student arrives in order to satisfy some burning internal drive. Many students come from well-heeled families comprised of judges and attorneys.

But Maxey arrived at this prestigious gathering with an outrageous backwater Okie accent, straight out of the southeastern Oklahoma hills. Even for Oklahoma, it was bad. Most of the Okie natives in their first year of law school had long since learned to mask their regional accent in academia. An Okie accent exists somewhere between a Western twang and a Louisiana drawl. But Maxey never put on airs. She made no effort to disguise her roots. In her own words, she was a "take them by the balls" kind of gal.

She struck a fetching sight in the crowd with her broad smile, white-blond hair and lithe figure. She was immediately dismissed as an intellectual threat by many of her classmates because she didn't study like the rest. The most serious students scheduled study time in the stately University of Oklahoma law library after class, foregoing family, work and other obligations to try and reach academic achievement amongst a college full of achievers. But no one ever spotted Maxey in the library. She preferred instead to socialize and sip on a pint with friends at the local pub. But the proficiency for lawyering she had displayed those years before never left her.

Each professor assigned volumes of required reading, including a daily case which had to be "briefed" for discussion just in case the student was selected to discuss it in front of her peers the next day. Sometimes the professor would be kind and genuine in pursuit of learning the law. Others were pointed, mean or belligerent toward the student selected to brief. This antagonistic environment, by design or in practice or both, proved too much for some, and several students dropped out due to the pressure. A weaker personality could be lost through the cracks. But that was the point. The first year served as an initiation of sorts and the process sought to weed out the weak. But Maxey was not one of those personalities. In fact, she thrived under fire. Her confidence grew with every public grilling that came her way. She met the older, more experienced professors with the same defiance and ornery self-determination she had developed as a young girl. It was the quality that would one day make her a worthy adversary in court against much older and experienced defense attorneys. Maxey Parker could not have known it then, but every challenge she met in law school prepared her for the greatest trial of her life, which lay some ten years in the future.

# CHAPTER 2

# Okfuskee County

*You know what blood looks like in a black and white video? Shadows. Shadows!*
~Lake Marie, John Prine

**W**eleetka is a small Oklahoma town situated ten miles southeast of Okemah, the Okfuskee county seat. The county's claim to fame is their most famous export, Woody Guthrie. Guthrie was the legendary traveling bard whose art influenced every major figure in Americana music and literature, including Bob Dylan, Bruce Springsteen and Will Rogers. John Steinbeck said of Guthrie, "Harsh voiced and nasal . . . there is nothing sweet about Woody, and there is nothing sweet about the songs he sings. But there is something more important for those who will listen." It is difficult to overstate the pervasive social impact of Woody's writing, singing and compositions, even fifty years after his death. He remains, to make a jaunty comparison, Oklahoma's Homer.

Okemah still celebrates Woody's birth every July. During a five-day music festival, everyday life in the small town comes to a full stop. Performance stages go up all over town and artists caravan in for a jubilee dedicated to Okfuskee County's favorite son. One of Woody's more light-hearted songs,

'Way Over Yonder in the Minor Key', serves as an affectionate nod to his Okfuskee County home:

*I lived in a place called Okfuskee*

*And I had a little girl in a holler tree*

*I said, little girl, it's plain to see*

*Ain't nobody that can sing like me*

*We walked down by the Buckeye Creek*

*To see the frog eat the goggle-eye bee*

*To hear the west wind whistle to the east*

*There ain't nobody that can sing like me*

But any student of Woody Guthrie knows, as Steinbeck pointed out, that many more Guthrie songs lament the living conditions of the working poor, blast the failure of the judicial system to achieve the promise of equal rights, and protest the dehumanization of immigrants and migrant workers. It is no coincidence then, that Woody Guthrie grew up in Okfuskee County and went on to sing about the social justice issues he witnessed all around.

The poverty Guthrie wrote about is a struggle with which many area residents remain familiar, even some eighty years later. The 2016 U.S. census reported that out of approximately one thousand people living in Okfuskee town boundaries, 48% of the households reported an income of $24,999 or less. Per capita income in town averaged $15,841, which left about 23% of families with children 18 or younger living below the poverty line.

But the economic outlook hadn't always been so bleak in Weleetka. There once was a golden age within its boundaries at the beginning of the twentieth century, as with many Oklahoma towns. The iron horse charged through, bringing with it visitors from afar, along with their dollars. Weleetka had a hotel then, and a number of other services to accommodate the railway and its men.

The railroad came in from Ft. Smith, Arkansas, and even boasted regular passenger service with Pullman sleeping cars moving to and from St. Louis and Oklahoma City. The lines served major mining operations in eastern Oklahoma. But the coal traffic would inevitably decline, leaving a vacuum in its absence. The decline was a slow one, but it came nonetheless. The railroad officially ended its run in Weleetka in 1939. By that time, young Woody Guthrie was long gone, but the place where he forged his youth cut deep in his psyche and stayed with him in song for the rest of his life.

Weleetka is the Creek Nation word for running water. It is an apt word since the place is located near the North Canadian River. Natives make up nearly a quarter of the population in Okfuskee County. It is a microcosm reflecting the state of Oklahoma itself. While American society at large recognizes the state as Indian Territory, the reasons for that have been lost, forgotten or repressed. The story certainly never held a place of prominence in public school history courses. The Native population within the boundaries of Oklahoma came to be, in large part, due to the systematic forced removal of sovereign tribes during the mid-1800s. During this time, the United States government forced Native people living in their homelands of the southeastern region of the country, to relocate to lands west of the Mississippi, land considered at that time to be devoid of value by White European settlers. The forced migration oftentimes during the harsh winters of the American South, meant a death sentence for thousands. The name Okfuskee comes from the Muskvgee tribe. The land was previously occupied by Quapaw and Osage tribes until 1825 when they ceded the land to the United States government.

After the United States violated the terms of several treaties with the Muskvgee, most of their people were removed to Indian Territory in 1834.

Andrew Jackson later addressed the nations forced from their ancestral homelands in what must surely rank as one of the most historically shameful and fraudulent missives ever composed by a U.S. President:

"Friends and Brothers - By permission of the Great Spirit above, and the voice of the people, I have been made President of the United States, and now speak to you as your Father and friend, and request you listen. Your warriors have known me long. You know I love my white and red children, and always speak with a straight, and not with a forked tongue; that I have always told you the truth ... Where you now are, you and my white children are too near to each other to live in harmony and peace. Your game is destroyed, and many of your people will not work and till the earth. Beyond the great River Mississippi, where a part of your nation has gone, your Father has provided a country large enough for all of you, and he advises you to remove to it. There your white brothers will not trouble you; they will have no claim to the land, and you can live upon it you and all your children, as long as the grass grows or the water runs, in peace and plenty. It will be yours forever. For the improvements in the country where you now live, and for all the stock which you cannot take with you, your Father will pay you a fair price ..."

~President Andrew Jackson, 1829

When the Native nations removed to Oklahoma they often brought slaves with them. When the Civil War was decided some of the newly freed men and women settled down in the same areas where they gained their freedom, founding all-black communities that remain to this day. One of those all-black communities settled in Okfuskee County. This was the site of an event that inspired yet another Woody Guthrie song. This time the subject was much more calamitous.

A crowd of men lynched a local woman and her son, Laura and L.D. Nelson, and hung them by their necks beneath a railroad bridge that spanned the Canadian River. A photograph was taken at the scene that showed at least fifty onlookers standing above the dead mother and son. No one came to claim their bodies after they were cut down from the bridge.

Guthrie's song referenced the event, singing, "dedicated to the many negro mothers and fathers, and sons alike, that was lynched and hanged under the bridge of the Canadian River, seven miles south of Okemah, Oklahoma, and to the day when such will be no more."

Rumors have long swirled that Guthrie's own father took part in the lynching that night. Woody himself would not be born for another three years after the lynching took place. But he would have heard the stories and seen the photograph taken that day, which became famous nationwide and remains the only photographic evidence of a lynched woman in the United States.

The details of what happened to Laura Nelson and L.D. Nelson must have affected Woody Guthrie to the core because he later composed a harrowing song about the event, called 'Don't Kill My Baby and My Son'.

The difficult and sometimes violent history of Okfuskee County commiserates well with stories from the other 77 counties. The state is populated by a gathering of refugees of sorts; in addition to the wide expanse of heritage forged by official policies of the 1800s, the Ozark foothills to the east once served as ideal hiding places for those seeking refuge from the long arm of the law, including famous names such as Jesse James and the James gang, Belle Starr and her children.

Today the resultant population includes a rich amalgam of survivors and non-conformists, rebels, artists, musicians and tragedians. It is a hearty, defiant and darkly humorous stock that managed to remain and thrive here. Maxey Parker decided to raise a family of her own right in the bittersweet, chaotic middle of it.

She first met Robert Reilly on a blind date arranged by mutual friends while she was still in law school. Robert hailed from Okemah, the well-to-do son of a successful local businessman. In his youth he was a bit of a freewheeler. He and a friend set out to tour Europe together after college, staying in hostels and working odd jobs for spending money. He hadn't committed to a profession yet and certainly wasn't sold on remaining in his old home town. But then Robert sat down with his father after college and agreed that he would one day run the family business. The Reilly family occupation strikes the population at large as an odd choice. It is a very strange pursuit of a profession. Theirs is the task no one wants to do and prays they will not need. But to the Reillys of Okemah, the role of town undertaker is neither bizarre nor unpleasant. The job might be undesired by most but it is a fine breadwinner in a small town. They are very good at what they do.

Robert is, at first meeting, a reserved and unassuming man. Tall, sandy-haired and lean, he conducts himself in the congenial manner expected of a funeral director. Rob carries himself with a demeanor that brings about a certain level of calm to any situation. He is a man with a natural gift for putting people at ease, even after the loss of a loved one. He maintains that same cool demeanor at home, albeit with a wry sense of humor he must understandably keep in check in the workplace. He is a bit of a dilettante chef, known locally for his wild game recipes and proclivity for barbecue competitions.

Their first date came about on St. Patrick's Day, 2001. Rob borrowed his sister's BMW for the occasion in an attempt to impress Maxey, and Maxey borrowed her own sister's car in an attempt to impress Robert. Robert had been drinking beer before her arrival that day in an attempt to calm his nerves before their first meeting. Unbeknownst to him, he walked out to greet her with Guinness dribbled down the front of his shirt. They went out on the town that night and got themselves kicked out of a bar. That was it for the both of them; they had found true love. Whereas some women might have been troubled by Robert's chosen profession,

Maxey thrived on the unconventional nature of his work. During one of their dates Robert transported a corpse to Tulsa. The hearse broke down on the side of Highway 75, right in front of the Creek Turnpike exit. The couple sat there stranded alongside their unfortunate passenger, waiting on rescue. People passed by and honked. Neither Maxey nor Rob considered their predicament awkward. They shared a common philosophy that even the most difficult circumstances provide for another day at the office. They are a hard working stock.

North of Okemah the main thoroughfare is a two lane state highway that winds around and eventually points toward Tulsa. But the environs outside Okemah couldn't be more removed from the big city and that is just how Maxey and Robert wanted it. They married on St. Patrick's Day, 2004 and Maxey Parker became Maxey Parker Reilly. She began her young prosecutorial career with the District Attorney's office in Okemah when the D.A. himself called to request that she join his office. In rural counties such as Okfuskee, it is common for the District Attorney to maintain one or two assistant district attorneys. Such was Maxey's beginning in the prosecutorial arena. She and Robert purchased a place in town situated within near-immediate commutes to their respective offices. They took the place knowing that at some point in the near future they would build a home out in the pastoral countryside where they both felt more comfortable.

A few miles outside of town, nestled in a dense protective forest, lies a little known lake. In a state where most residents load up the family on the weekend to boat, fish and sun on the banks of sprawling lakes such as Texoma, Eufaula and Grand, Lake Okemah is a much more serene alternative. Few Oklahomans know of its existence outside Okfuskee county. A hundred miles of country lanes encircle this quaint but beautiful body of water. It is difficult for a newcomer to gain her bearings, even after multiple visits. Fine, isolated, upper-middle class homes stand on its shores along with a few fixer-uppers and even a couple of abandoned properties. The residents there like it that way.

Maxey and Robert Reilly settled on the spot after searching for the perfect place to raise a little brood. Driving along mostly dirt roads, they turned down a lane so narrow, so remote, they felt certain it must end in the lake. But they continued on until it wound around and turned downhill. When they reached the end there sat a quaint but lovely cabin, with a glorious full deck that faced directly out to a fishing dock, a mere hundred yards away. Together the Reillys surveyed the broad, unobscured view of the lake, the dense protection of the surrounding woods, the sparkling invitation of the water, and they knew they had found the ideal home where they would raise their children. The couple considered the place a vacation spot and a home all at once. On hot summer days families stayed out skiing across the lake's smooth surface from sunup to sundown. They knew it would make a wonderful place for children to grow up.

Life on the lake is decidedly laid back. Fog rolls across the water while ducks glide in under cover. Pelicans gather to confer on a small island in the center of the lake. The people who settle around its shores prize their individuality, but they also share some core values: privacy, hunting (and therefore firearms), roots music and a drink. The only real way to spy on a neighbor is to get on a dinghy and head across the lake. The residents don't see much need for fences since the trees and thick underbrush provide daunting boundaries between properties. Maxey saw in the area a chance to pick back up on her old school hunting and fishing habits. In its isolation she also saw the opportunity for an escape from the pressures of her job as the local prosecutor.

An A.D.A.'s work is intense, with long hours away from home, particularly during trial preparation. Part of the job includes fielding aggressive accusations from the community, sometimes infuriated by the prosecution of a loved one. More than once Maxey left the courthouse to find her tires slashed. In an adjoining county someone left a pipe bomb in a car outside the courthouse. Maxey worked with an acute awareness that some of these people were her neighbors and that inevitably she would have to put some of them in jail. The responsibility proved a difficult tightwire to toe in a small town. Once in a while the pressure was enough to move her to tears. She never let anyone see that part of the job. During those times she retreated to her place down by the lake. It gave her sanctuary, a solid rock.

She chose her friends carefully and kept them close to the vest. The ones who stuck demonstrated loyalty and a disinterest in gossip. Enough whispers already circulated around town to satisfy the local rumor mill. One of those in her circle of trust was a fellow lake resident who soon became her best friend, a bubbly woman named Claudia. Every fall Claudia hosted a "Doe Party" and invited Maxey. They called themselves "Doe Widows" because their men would leave out for deer camp where, historically speaking, women were not invited.

Claudia, shiny and bright in a tiara and tap shoes, hosted these peculiar occasions out in the woods. A caravan of women would file in, dressed in costume. They assigned each other names such as Jane Doe, Doe Rito, etc. Maxey's name was The Doe-strict Attorney. They gathered in a cabin with animal heads peering down from the walls, complete with cheap wine, great tubs of iced-down cold beer and carefully chosen records to set the mood for a country party. More often than not the preferred tunes came from favored local sons like

John Fullbright, the Turnpike Troubadours and Woody.

Claudia lived in a lake house just down the lane from Maxey's and she proved a fast and loyal confidante. Her vibrant personality complimented Maxey's wry one. She had already lived a life worthy of a book by the time they became friends. Claudia had been once divorced when she met her true love, a man named Ronnie. She found in Ronnie a kindred spirit who also embraced the lake philosophy. He held an exuberant passion for life, unlike any of them had ever seen before. They made a cozy but adventurous life together out in the woods. Maxey and Robert, Claudia and Ronnie became fast friends.

It was not unusual for Ronnie to go hunting with the guys for several days at a time, so it came as no surprise when he packed up his gear and took off for an excursion in the Missouri backcountry. Claudia never imagined for a moment that her second chance at love would be cut short. But that weekend Ronnie missed a turn while riding his ATV and slammed into a tree. Rob and Maxey were at home when they received a call from a mutual friend who had come upon the tragic scene. When she heard the news Maxey sunk to her knees on the cold tile of the bathroom floor and wept for Ronnie's loss. She also wept for the grief she knew her best friend would now face. But there would be much more grief to come in Okfuskee County. Soon, the new prosecutor would be tasked

with hunting down the killer of two little girls from
just down the road.

# CHAPTER 3

## They Killed Our Babies

*Shall I go now? Down that road no one knows*
*And shall I go into the night?*
*This is your reality, not mine*
~While I'm Young, Lauren Barth

The two girls were extremely close, even though they were separated in age by two years. Their weekends were busy with slumber parties just as often as the adults would allow. Taylor Placker's grandparents often hosted the sleepovers at their modest home located just south of Bad Creek Bridge on County Line Road.

Taylor's grandparents, Peter and Vicky Placker, enjoyed a rather typical Saturday afternoon on the 7th of June, 2008. He watched television and she played games on the computer. Just like every Oklahoma day in June, it was hot out. Very hot. The family had their AC window unit running at full blast, battling the heat waves that pushed through the front door every time the girls ran in and out.

The house was rather small, in line with most of the other homes located along the road. It was nestled beside a trio of oak trees that sheltered the home from prairie winds. County Line Road served as the dividing line between Okfuskee and Okmulgee counties. The Placker family home was located on the Okfuskee side. The road ran directly in front of their property although the home itself sat a good hundred yards back. All along the ditch in front of the home grew thickets of purple irises, standing in proud contrast to their plaintive surroundings. No other homes could be seen from the Placker place.

Despite the diminutive size of the home, a mere 1200 square feet, several members of the Placker family lived in the dwelling besides Taylor and her grandparents. Their two adult daughters, Linda and Jennifer, also called the place home.

The Placker family had lived in the area for three years in the summer of 2008, having moved there from Oklahoma City in 2005. Peter worked as a mechanic in Oklahoma City and then decided to move his family out to the country in large part to raise young Taylor in the peaceful environs of a rural area, away from the concrete hustle of the city. They had only been living in the County Line residence for a year. It is not uncommon for family members to take up residence near each other in Oklahoma and so it was with the Plackers. Peter's brothers, Charles and Darrell, lived just down the road. A few of the immediate family members had felony convictions but that never bothered Peter. Most families in Oklahoma brag about their "outlaw" family connections. A common, sentimental joke often used to refer to family reunions in the state is said to be a gathering of "in-laws and outlaws".

Peter and Vicky Taylor were technically Taylor's grandparents but they had raised her as their own daughter from the day she was born. Their daughter Jennifer had given birth to Taylor but by all accounts lived as Taylor's big sister rather than her mother. Taylor's biological father had only met her twice in her thirteen years and so Peter was the steady male figure in her life. Taylor called Peter and Vicky her mom and dad. She called her birth mother by 'Jenny' and regarded her as a big sister, although Taylor knew the truth about her biological parents.

Taylor was quiet and shy. She was taller than most of the class, boys and girls both. Her eyes were dark and serious beneath cropped bangs. Before she transferred into Graham Public Schools her family saw that she received her education in the home. She wanted to be a forensic scientist when she grew up. She was considered the smartest in her class. Taylor was, perhaps more than anything else, an avid animal lover. A grand total of eight dogs followed along as she explored the rural countryside. The girl demanded her family stop the car any time she spotted a turtle on the road. She routinely jumped out and carried them out of the road to grassy freedom. Sometimes she wrote her name on the tops of their shells before she turned them back to the wild.

Her shy nature did not deter an eagerness to bring joy to the people around her. The bus driver remembered her walking to the bus with a smile on her face every day. She was elected elementary school queen when she sold the most raffle tickets for fundraising. Taylor was friendly and popular with all her classmates as a sixth grader at nearby Graham public school. But only one person ranked as her best friend, only one girl with whom she spent most of her free time and shared her innermost secrets. That girl was Skyla Whitaker.

Skyla was a freckled tomboy who loved to fish. Her budding interests included rocketry and quilting. She was a skinny extrovert with a playful light in her eyes. Her family lived in a rural area outside Henryetta, a larger town farther east on Interstate 40 from Weleetka. She was the daughter of James and Rose Whitaker. She was the middle sister of three girls. On occasion she liked to stir up a row with her sisters. Like Taylor, she was crazy about animals. Skyla's animals likewise followed her around wherever she went, including "five or six cats...her little dog and her goat." She preferred to roam barefoot. An adventurer, she careened her bicycle up and down the backroads. She moved to Okfuskee County from Baxter Springs, Kansas with her mother and step-father. Like the Plackers, Skyla's family had seen its fair share of trouble as well. Skyla's older brother had been arrested and took a plea deal in the shooting death of a celebrated athlete back in Kansas. Their move to Oklahoma served, in part, to escape the family stigma of the crime.

At thirteen, Taylor did not yet have a boyfriend, although she was beginning to develop crushes on some of the boys she saw on television. She had saved up her money and purchased a cell phone for herself a couple of months earlier. She carried it with her wherever she went.

Besides the occasional boy crush, Taylor followed suit of typical Okie girls in other ways, too. She loved to explore. The vast prairielands provide an endless natural amusement park where an adventurous youngster can wander for hours and never become bored. The hayfields are populated by heifers and newborn calves, galloping horses and braying mules. Great soaring eagles and red hawks cast their shadows below. Little streams crisscross the grasslands. They sometimes remain hidden until you walk right up on them. These streams are the most magical places, the "secret places" where an imaginative child can swing her feet off a fallen log and peer down at bullfrog tadpoles flitting back and forth in the water below. In these places a girl can spend hours dreaming of the years to come, imagining herself as a grown up, falling in love and exploring the world outside the confines of the little place where she'd been raised. It is a chance to dream of the great adventures that lie beyond the borders of a small town. Taylor enjoyed these places and regularly carried a fishing pole in search of a nice fishing hole and some time alone to dream.

Both Taylor and Skyla attended Graham public school, which in 2008 described itself as a rural consolidated school ten miles south of Henryetta. The school was so small as to allow for just one classroom to accommodate both 5th and 6th grades. As such, the girls were able to be in the same classroom together despite their age difference. Perhaps on paper Skyla and Taylor appeared to be polar opposites. But theirs was a strong connection, knitted together by deep mutual esteem. They both loved to read. The school librarian reported that there was hardly a book left in Graham's entire collection that had not been checked out by one or both of the girls. They painted each other's fingernails and drew tattoos on each other in marker. They both joined the cheerleading squad. Skyla played for the basketball team.

After Taylor transferred into Graham Public Schools the two girls had sleepovers at least a dozen times in that first year. Most of the time Skyla would go over to the Placker house. During their slumber parties the girls turned the old shed behind the house into their very own clubhouse. They giggled and whispered to each other in Taylor's bedroom and at night they sometimes played games together on the shared family computer.

The weekend of June 8th, Skyla went to spend the night with Taylor once again. That Saturday evening there were four people in the home: Peter and Vicky, Taylor and Skyla. Jennifer left out for Tulsa that weekend to visit her other child. As soon as Skyla arrived that afternoon the girls scuttled off on their own. They played in Taylor's room until they were ready to go explore outside. As per their usual routine the girls left the house and made the short walk down to the bridge, located just a half mile north of the Placker home. The girls had made the trek many times before. Taylor walked up to the bridge almost every single day. It was a chance to get out of the house for some space and privacy, a peaceful respite. The rocks crunched underfoot as they made their way toward the bridge. From time to time they spotted a vehicle parked up there. Taylor made a habit of turning around and heading back in the opposite direction any time she saw a parked vehicle. She preferred to enjoy the creek alone if Skyla couldn't be with her. The bridge was so close to the Placker home that anyone with good eyesight could walk out into the road and see it. That Saturday the girls took their time in the summer heat, walking the distance down to the creek and back in a span of forty-five minutes.

It was a very familiar routine for Taylor. Thirteen is a challenging age for girls and Taylor had begun to use the word "pudgy" to describe her own body. She made up her mind to exercise back and forth to the bridge daily. She had a habit of kicking rocks off the side of the bridge once she arrived, watching them splash in the shallow waters that ran just twenty feet below. Skyla accompanied her friend on the walk, as she always had, on that Saturday in June.

Vicky Placker typically slept on the well-worn couch in front of the television while Peter often retired to their bedroom at nighttime. Their adult daughter Linda slept in her own room and Taylor had a little adjoining room which she claimed as her own. But that Saturday night Peter let the little girls have his room while he went out to sleep near his wife by the comforting din of late night television. The girls stayed up into the wee hours of the morning, long after the adults had fallen asleep in the living room. The next day, on Sunday, they slept in past the morning when Peter and Vicky got around to start their day. Vicky began by firing up the computer. She enjoyed passing the time with online games. Peter settled in front of the television.

After their extremely late night the girls didn't stir until late into Sunday afternoon; 3 p.m. or so. They played around outside after they got up and then came inside to inquire about taking one more walk down to Bad Creek Bridge. Taylor never left on one of her walks without asking permission first and that Sunday was no exception. Peter, somewhat distracted by Nascar races on television, told the girls it was fine to go on down to the bridge and turned his attention back to the race.

Taylor made a habit of collecting the occasional curiosity she discovered on her walks, so she liked to carry a backpack for just such an opportunity. She picked up the various spent shell casings that could be found any given time on that particular road. It was not unusual for passersby to shoot off their firearms from the road at nothing in particular and leave the casings behind. The gun culture is a strong and ever-present part of the rural Okie identity. The sound of gunfire strikes no one as reason for any particular concern on Oklahoma back roads. Taylor carried a bottle of water and her cell phone as a matter of habit in her backpack. Her dogs followed after the girls.

Not more than ten minutes after they left Peter's phone rang. It was Rose Whitaker, Skyla's mother, calling to say she was on her way from Henryetta to pick up her daughter. Peter and Vicky immediately called Taylor's phone to tell the girls to turn back around and head home. Skyla would need to get her things together so that her mother would not have to wait on her. But Vicky got no response from Taylor.

It was not unusual for cell service in that area to be very spotty. It was possible to walk two feet in one direction and have no service at all, then move two feet in the opposite direction and have calls go through with no problem. But this time, even after walking out into the middle of County Line Road, Vicky could not reach Taylor on her phone. Vicky craned her neck looking for the girls as she dialed, hoping to spot them someplace down the road but she couldn't see anything at all. She finally gave up and hollered at Peter. Peter walked out into the road as well, and when he couldn't spot the girls he hurried back into the house and put his shoes on. He went back out and began to walk toward the bridge. He and Vicky wanted to make sure the girls were back safe at the house by the time Skyla's mother arrived from Henryetta.

Peter began walking north around 5:15 p.m. He didn't feel that anything in particular was the matter, other than the fact that from where he walked he couldn't see the girls. But he could see the bridge. He hadn't made it more than half the distance to the bridge, about a quarter of a mile, when he walked right up on Taylor and Skyla lying in the ditch.

He would later describe it by saying, "I walked almost on them before I saw them."

They were lying in the ditch on the west side of the road, the Okfuskee side. His granddaughter, the girl he had raised as his own daughter since her birth, was lying crossways in the ditch. Her head had fallen to the west with her body stretching across the depression in the ground. Her feet pointed toward the east. Her best friend Skyla lay just above on the craggy embankment that rose slightly from the road. At first sight of the girls, Peter believed that a passing motorist must have struck them and thrown them out of the road. He knelt down next to his daughter and pressed his fingertips against the inside of her wrist but found no pulse. Desperate, he then reached to Skyla and felt her arm for life in the same way. Nothing. It was then that Mr. Placker walked back out to the middle of County Line Road, just down the way from Bad Creek Bridge. He faced in the direction of the place where he had raised and cared for his family of girls, and in his own words, Peter Placker began to scream his head off.

Taylor's cell phone continued to sound off in her bag as she lay dead in the ditch. Her grandmother had continued to call even as her husband was struggling with the realization of what it meant that blood no longer pulsed through Taylor's veins. Peter screamed at Vicky from the middle of the road pleading for her to call the authorities. He then went back to Taylor's body, reached into her backpack, grabbed her cell phone and began trying to call 911 though he never made a connection. He next attempted to call his brother Charles, who lived just down the road, for help, but Charles did not answer. At last, Peter was able to make contact with someone to convey the desperate scene that lay at his feet. His daughter Linda was on her way home from working a shift at Arby's. When she answered her father's call Mr. Placker had just four words to describe the event that would change all their lives forever: "They killed our babies."

The scene along County Line Road turned to chaos after Peter discovered Taylor and Skyla in the ditch. The first vehicle to drive up on the scene was his daughter Linda. Peter waved her through. Immediately following Linda was Peter's younger brother Darrell. Linda stopped the car right next to the place where her little sister had fallen. Peter Placker demanded she keep her eyes on him.

"Look at me. Look at me," he pled with her. "Go get your mama."

Linda followed Peter's instructions and drove on to the house to find her mother, who had not yet been down to the scene.

Peter directed his brother Darrell to park his van sideways in the roadway to block access to the site. Shortly thereafter, a gray pickup approached from the south. Peter began to walk in the direction of the small truck to request that it block approaching traffic. He didn't realize until he walked up to the truck that the driver was Rose Whitaker, Skyla's mother. She had just arrived to pick up her daughter. She was completely unaware of her daughter's condition. Rose stepped out of her truck. Peter said to her, "They're gone, they're both gone. The girls are dead." Once again, he uttered the same phrase he had said to his daughter over the phone. "They killed our babies," and Rose began to scream.

She made an attempt to go to her daughter but Peter would not allow it. Rose reached into her truck, Peter feared for her keys, so he reached in and took the keys from the ignition. But Rose was reaching for her cell phone to call for her husband.

An ambulance came screaming down County Line from the north. Three paramedics exited and Peter asked them to check the girls again for a pulse. The older paramedic of the three checked both of the girls then looked up. "They're gone," he said. The girls were covered with sheets retrieved from the Placker household. After that Peter's life became a blur. His brother Charles arrived on the scene followed by the first succession of law enforcement vehicles, then concerned neighbors and more family. Peter turned and walked away from the scene having done everything he could for the girls. He knew there was no more he could do except to allow the authorities to do their jobs.

Several hours after the crime scene was established, Maxey Parker Reilly's phone rang. Maxey's baby boy had been born just a few months earlier. The little Reilly family of three had retired to the couch for a relaxed Sunday evening. She took the call and recognized the voice of her colleague Kurt Titsworth. Kurt was one of the investigators who worked with the District Attorney's office. He was calling from a murder scene. The information she received over the phone wasn't very detailed. She only understood that a double homicide had occured near Weleetka and that children were possibly involved. Maxey called her boss, the District Attorney, to let him know they were needed immediately. She pulled on her clothes, strapped on her pistol and kissed her husband goodbye. She told him not to wait up. From the sound of it, she thought, this one might take a while.

# CHAPTER 4

# Long Days After

*I still call that town my heart*
*Though I've left and I still roam*
*Can't explain just how I felt*
*Living in the Bible belt.* ~Bible Belt, Kalyn Fay Barnoski

ADA Reilly arrived on the Weleetka crime scene after the O.S.B.I. had already begun to process the murder scene. As prosecutor, she had a delicate responsibility to avoid interfering as law enforcement went about their work. But it was also important to monitor evidence collection and processing. She knew from previous missteps that respectful oversight would make her job easier when it came time to present the case in court. When she and the District Attorney arrived she noted a man sitting in a police car. As she worked the case she would later come to know him as Peter Placker. She and the D.A. approached the crime scene tape and noted a large crowd of onlookers standing there, shoulder to shoulder, clamoring for a look at the scene. An officer stood nearby with a short list of names that he used to grant access past the yellow tape. Maxey showed her identification to the officer and entered the cordoned-off area.

Within the perimeter Agent Brad Green and two other investigators from the Oklahoma State Bureau of Investigation were already at work.

Green received notification of the murders around 6:15 p.m. He had immediately jumped in his truck and drove just over two hours to Okfuskee County. He arrived at approximately 8:30 p.m. Due to the long summer days it was still light out but the sun was beginning to set. The fire department brought in artificial lighting for the crime scene work that would go on throughout the night. An occasional breeze moved through the trees and provided some relief from the heat.

Agent Green began his normal procedures for processing a crime scene. He took extensive photographs. Then he identified, collected, and packaged potential evidence. He documented evidence at the scene with small, yellow placards. He and the other agents processed the area through the night. Among the items they submitted as evidence: five spent Winchester .40 caliber hulls that were found by a paramedic in the roadway, the sheets that covered the bodies of the two girls, a nearby keychain and a discarded Mountain Dew can, which was located about fifty feet north of the bodies.

Green also collected a water bottle and Taylor's backpack from the scene. He noted three .12 gauge shotgun shell casings in the backpack. The majority of the other discarded shells were found approximately eight feet from Taylor's body.

The girls were found some nine hundred and sixty seven feet north of the Placker home on the west side of the road, which ran north and south. Taylor lay in the small bar ditch which had an incline on each side. Her feet were positioned on the incline that came down off of the roadway and into the bar ditch. Her legs were bent at the knees and spread apart. Her torso was mostly in the flat part of the ditch and her head was inclined. Skyla was located approximately four feet to the west of Taylor. She was found lying on her back, although her body was twisted somewhat. Investigators speculated that she had been in the process of turning to run for her life when she fell. Her head faced back toward the west and her body was up on the hill area. The top of the hill was covered with weeds, trees and brush. A barbed wire fence ran along the top of the hill. Skyla's body was just a few feet from that fence. Both girls were found fully clothed.

The wounds were numerous and cruel. Taylor had been shot on the left side of her chin, once above her lip and below the nose on the left side of her face. Another bullet struck the right side of her cheek and her right hand. The final gunshot entered her left groin area. Two of the wounds to her face were noticeably smaller. The shots that entered her groin, hand and right cheek appeared to be larger than the rest. Agent Green surmised right away that a minimum of two guns had been used. It appeared to him that Taylor had raised her hand in an attempt to block the bullet because it had traveled through her hand and into her cheek.

Skyla also suffered multiple injuries. Her shirt on the left side appeared to be burned where one of the bullets entered her body. She suffered several wounds on the right side. The investigators noted blood near her armpit and on her sleeve. There was an entry wound inside her right arm. Skyla's neck was struck by a bullet just below the chin. Agent Green surmised that these bullets also came from a smaller caliber weapon. There was no visible blood at the neck wound, which indicated to investigators that the injury was inflicted either post mortem or very close to death. The onslaught told a story to the investigating agents that the shooter was not satisfied with murder. He had been intent on overkill.

The injury to Taylor's groin was of particular interest to detectives. An examination revealed no bullet holes or burn marks in the shorts she had worn that day, but they found a bullet wound to her groin, underneath the shorts. Agent Green noted that he didn't see any blood around the groin wound. He surmised that if the shot had happened while Taylor was standing up he would have expected to find blood dripping from the wound or on the ground, but he did not find any blood from the groin.The only way that particular wound could have been inflicted was if 1) the girl had been shot in the groin without shorts on and then someone had put her shorts back on over the wound or 2) the shot was taken after the girl had already fallen into the ditch with her legs bent up in the position she was found in death, allowing the bullet to pass under the shorts without damaging them.

After working the scene all night, Agent Green left the next morning around 9:30 a.m. The Placker family met with investigators multiple times in the days after the killings. One of the first officials with whom Peter interviewed was Kurt Titsworth. The detective was a handsome, genial man with an easy smile. He was a small town fellow who grew up with a passion for law enforcement. Titsworth became the agent to work most closely with the family over the course of the investigation. He would be the one to deliver the breaks, or lack of them, as things turned out. The family racked their brains to search for some sort of motive to aid the investigation but in truth they could not imagine anyone capable of such an atrocity against their little girl. The authorities confiscated the Placker's computer and a rifle that Mr. Placker kept under his bed. They took some of Taylor's clothing and a comforter for analysis.

The press swarmed the area and the Plackers made an attempt to oblige them early on, hoping their cooperation and visibility to the public might be of some use. Peter was in such an emotional state that he could not bring himself to repeat specific details about walking up on the girls that day. Still, he and other family members put up a brave front and called on anyone with information to come forward.

The O.S.B.I. had no real leads to move on, although officials began to speculate that the murderer would likely be a local resident familiar with the area. An apparent lack of motive continued to baffle authorities. Theories ranged from a random thrill kill to the possibility that the girls may have interrupted criminal activity on the road.

The quaint Weleetka community and surrounding areas became more and more fearful at each passing day without an arrest. Statements of disbelief and shock echoed in the press from educators, parents and even law enforcement, all of whom agreed with the general sentiment that "this kind of thing just doesn't happen here."

After a drenching rain on Monday the County Commissioners ordered the road graded. By Tuesday, the murder site was transformed into a large, makeshift memorial. Mourners came bearing stuffed animals, dolls, crosses and flowers to mark the tragic spot.  County authorities warned the community that they still did not know exactly how to describe the potential threat. It seemed unlikely that a random person would find his way to County Line Road from the interstate or nearby Highway 75. The sheriff advised parents to keep close watch over their children. A reward for information leading to an arrest grew to $14,000.

Even though summer break had only just gone into full swing, parents kept their children indoors, fearing a predator on the loose. Many residents kept firearms at the ready, determined to defend their own should the need arise. Concerned mothers and fathers kept the phone ringing day and night at the sheriff's office. Rumors ran rampant. One of the many theories posited that the girls walked up on an illicit drug deal gone wrong. Another supposed a deranged shooter on a random murder spree.

Though the finality of burial seemed unimaginable to the families, plans began to emerge for funeral services to be held once the Medical Examiner's Office in Oklahoma City returned their bodies. Taylor's service came five days later, at the Dewar First Baptist church just outside Henryetta. The family arranged for an open casket covered with pink and white carnations. The preacher's message called for the community to come together. He urged people to believe that something good could eventually come from tragedy.

A few hours later another pastor relayed a similar message at Skyla's funeral wherein he implored hundreds of his fellows to find a way to become "better, not bitter". Skyla's sister, Rosita, stood before the congregants and read words written by their grieving mother:

*"Now she will never graduate … never have boyfriends … never go to college … never have children. Someone stole that from her …*

*What little comfort we have is that, in the end, she was with her best friend; walking, having a good time on a beautiful day."*

The messages calling for solidarity were heeded by most in the community. Classmates from Graham school took donation jars to surrounding businesses. A local church with only thirty-five congregants organized a fundraiser with baked goods and Indian tacos. A benefit barbecue and auction sold off horses and trailers, gasoline gift certificates and big screen televisions, all to fund the grieving families. Marvin's Place, a local beer joint in Henryetta, also brought scores together to raise money.

"The unique thing about this town is that it's culturally diverse," one member of a local congregation said to a reporter. "It has been since the very beginning and when something like this happens, it helps them come together as a family, so we can take care of our own family. It brings you together when you do things like this."

Law enforcement continued their tireless efforts even as the families solemnized their grief at the two funerals. That Friday as the girls were laid to rest officials described a person of interest whom they said was wanted for questioning, but not necessarily a suspect. Agents gathered and photographed mourners as they exited the church.

They took the visitor's registry from the funeral for reference. The agency released information that emerged from some of the interviews the O.S.B.I. conducted in the days after the murders. Witnesses reported seeing an American Indian man, 6 feet tall, with brown eyes and a long black ponytail driving a white Ford or Chevy pickup. They each reported that the man acted suspiciously, and had used his truck to block the road around the same time as the shooting. The account was corroborated by six witnesses according to an O.S.B.I. spokesperson.

The O.S.B.I. sketch proved a difficult prospect for the community. "American Indian, possibly Caucasian mixed" described a near majority of the population in Okfuskee County. Authorities began getting calls such as, "there's an Indian at the Conoco in Wagoner." When the O.S.B.I. spokesperson described the person of interest, she stated that witnesses reported he looked as if he didn't belong in the area. This, of course, was a conundrum considering the fact that Oklahoma is home to a much higher percentage of Native Americans than most other states.

Predictably, tips poured in as soon as the public viewed the sketch. The O.S.B.I. soon found itself overwhelmed with leads. The team had to devise a system to keep track of every tip and document when the tip had been "run out", as they called it. The public reward reached upwards of $30,000. Two private individuals from the oil and gas industry donated a $100,000 reward. By the time the two week mark approached, law enforcement set up roadblocks near Bad Creek Bridge to try and throw out a dragnet. Authorities stopped approximately 90 vehicles and reported two dozen tips, but none of them yielded actionable information.

Investigators questioned fifty people and investigated between one hundred fifty and two hundred leads within the first week following the murders. They employed lie detector tests and searched out residents with known criminal backgrounds. The first inklings of evidence began to appear in the press, including truck tracks and bullet casings found at the scene.

Uneasy residents took to police scanners, monitoring the radio waves for any sign of a break in the search for the killer. Even the slightest rumored activity sent the area into an uproar. Ten days after the murders, with no suspects in sight, police received a call about a domestic disturbance at the school. A distraught man was outside threatening to kill himself. The Oklahoma Highway Patrol received a message that a hostage crisis was taking place. But nothing of the sort ever occurred. An emotionally unstable and ill-timed parent was taken into custody outside the school without further ado. Once again the nervous community had to settle in and wait for an answer.

Law enforcement was quick to point out to unsettled residents that of the 55 investigators employed by the state of Oklahoma, 15 were assigned to the Weleetka murders. The O.S.B.I. returned on Thursday to conduct a grid search of the area. The Oklahoma Highway Patrol flew overhead and took aerial photographs. The O.S.B.I. along with the District Attorney's office created a designated "War Room" at the Okfuskee County Courthouse in a jury room. It served as ground zero for all incoming leads and the central gathering place for detectives, police and prosecutors. Officials set up a bank of computers and staffed them with researchers. Maxey Reilly and Kurt Titsworth became permanent fixtures in the War Room.

A month later, the initial furor had reduced down to a simmer. But residents remained on edge and any bit of news set the place back to boiling again. Someone stopped by the murder site and reported that one of the memorial crosses had been desecrated. The O.S.B.I. declined to release the exact wording found scrawled over the cross, but in effect the message was "you'll never catch me." Paranoia once again reached fever-pitch. The O.S.B.I. told the press that investigators did not believe the cruel act of vandalism would amount to a break in the case. They nonetheless collected the cross for handwriting and DNA analysis, despite skepticism of the potential results, especially given the large number of visitors who had been given free access to the memorial in the days immediately following the crime.

Locals began to pine for a return to normal. Some of the details they read in the press about their small town did not ring entirely true. They found it distasteful and offensive that the press mentioned the local methamphetamine problem. A debate broke out among residents about whether or not people regularly took target practice off of Bad Creek Bridge. People began to express a desire for the churning rumor mill to grind to a halt. They tired of maintaining constant vigilance. After all, no community can remain on high alert for too long without growing weary. Neighbors who lived near the bridge hoped the questions from outsiders would die down at last and focus could move back to their own lives. It didn't help matters that the local school children, who had been cooped up for almost the entirety of their summer break, began to protest and demand their freedom.

By the time September rolled around and school was back in session the leads that had once poured in after the release of the sketch began to falter. The O.S.B.I. determined that it would cut back the number of officers working the investigation from fifteen to four full time agents. Despite the cut in personnel, the law enforcement officials who remained at the War Room allowed for no decrease in their collective zeal to search out the killer. They launched an unprecedented hunt for the weapons in particular.

The O.S.B.I. sent out letters to every registered Glock owner in the area. Out of the sixty letters sent out, around forty area Glock owners voluntarily handed their guns over for test-firing. At the very least, since a suspect had not yet been brought in, they could begin to rule everyone else out. That Oklahoma residents would voluntarily hand over their guns for ballistics analysis was a revelatory statement on how the murders affected the population to its core. Rural Oklahoma culture is by and large suspicious of governmental authority insofar as private firearms are concerned. Many families hunt every season for both sport and food. The people are fiercely protective of their guns and their right to maintain them. Still, in response to the O.S.B.I. request they came out in scores to offer up their guns for testing. Hundreds of locals voluntarily gave up DNA samples for comparison to DNA recovered from the discarded Mountain Dew can on the scene. The people wanted justice and soon.

The case had not gone cold but it certainly had begun to cool off. By September the O.S.B.I. partnered with Lamar Advertising and Oklahoma Crime Stoppers to erect two billboards on I-40, the busy thoroughfare that ran west and east several miles from the crime scene. Investigators, who had painstakingly eliminated all meaningful leads, could only hope that some regular commuter from the area might view the billboards as a daily sign to give up information they knew or suspected that would solve the murders.

An O.S.B.I. spokesperson said, "We've always believed that someone close to the killers knows something, and hopefully the billboard will wear on them to the point that they come forward and help solve this case." That billboard was how most Oklahomans would remember the little girls for eight long years after the murders. Taylor and Skyla; two smiling faces on a giant billboard by the interstate, frozen in time, waiting for justice.

The Plackers left their family home on County Line Road two months after the murders. They never returned. The house caught fire not long after and was never rebuilt. The blackened shell of it stands there still, a burned out witness to echoing grief.

# CHAPTER 5

## No Known Suspects

*Out in the country where I used to roam*
*Up and down dirt roads I was never alone*
*There's a town in Oklahoma*
*I used to call home*
*~Town in Oklahoma, Wink Burcham*

The pressure on law enforcement did not relent as autumn arrived. Press coverage and public interest continued to mount unlike any previous crime the O.S.B.I. had encountered. As the foliage began to turn from green to fiery reds and oranges, officials cautioned that an effective investigation could not be rushed. The agency's spokesperson continually assured the public that a thorough investigation had to be conducted in order to survive the court system with a successful prosecution.

Special Agent Ben Rosser called a press conference at the Okfuskee County Courthouse to emphasize that the agency was still analyzing pieces of evidence collected at the scene, including ballistics and DNA.

Rosser called the conference to quell rumors and confusion. Some believed the killer or killers were already in custody and that a confession had been given. One woman falsely claimed that a man matching the O.S.B.I. sketch had broken into her home. Residents gathered alongside the press corps, eager to learn of progress. They were left deflated after receiving the news that no suspects had yet been identified.

Agents began to seek out the girls' classmates in an attempt to learn their habits and associates. They continued to process family computers and electronics. Several of them had been shared among the girls and their family members. A specially trained Labrador Retriever with the Bureau of Alcohol, Tobacco, Firearms and Explosives searched the Bad Creek area again for bullets and casings but turned up nothing. Someone called in a tip reporting a truck full of boys in the area at the time of the shootings. The boys, when interviewed, admitted to being in the area with a shotgun but were quickly eliminated as suspects. "They told us they were down there shooting, just like they would have been on any Sunday," Agent Rosser said.

The community experienced a moment of temporary relief when the District Attorney announced that a grand jury would interview three suspects. The first boy testified before the grand jury for two hours. He had found himself tangled up in considerable trouble over the months leading up to, and after, the shootings. Nicknamed Spud, the boy had attended the same school as the little girls several years earlier, but transferred to nearby Henryetta in the ninth grade. Family members filed for protective orders against him just two months prior to June 8, after claiming he threatened to burn their house down. Then just three weeks after the murders he was charged with burglary after allegedly breaking into a private residence.

Spud's buddy, 19, also testified that day, for about an hour. His parents feared that members of the community might attack their son out of ill-placed vengeance. They claimed he had already been threatened multiple times. The young man claimed to have heard the gunshots, but denied that he saw anything related to the killings that day. He told investigators that he had been at a friend's house and later went with them to Wal Mart shortly after the time of the murders.

Another man told agents he had seen the little girls shortly before the murders as they were playing in the front yard of the Placker home. He reported that he witnessed them together as he drove to his home on County Line Road, about eight miles away from the scene. His girlfriend confirmed the story. The man came under suspicion after someone noticed dark, red stains on his clothing. He maintained that the stains came from a woodworking project and test results confirmed that fact. He angrily proclaimed his innocence to the press as he awaited the grand jury while the other two suspects maintained silence. Several reports came in about a four wheel drive or an off road vehicle in use near the area at the time of the murders. Investigators checked out both men identified as operating the four wheelers and cleared them as suspects.

None of these leads produced a suspect and the O.S.B.I. went back to square one.

The defaced memorial cross also failed to provide further clues. The O.S.B.I. spokesperson said the agency believed meddlesome kids had written the message on the cross for attention. Inside the county courthouse pictures of evidence covered the walls of the War Room. They kept the investigative command center largely out of media view. Officials tacked a map of County Line Road and the bridge prominently on the wall.

Maxey spent every day combing over possible leads and theories with O.S.B.I. agents and other investigators assigned to the War Room. One of the law enforcement colleagues with whom she worked the most was Agent Titsworth; the investigator who had first spoken with the Placker family after the murders. He had just entered church on that Sunday evening of the murders. He never kept his phone on in church service. A local police officer interrupted the service to call the detective out.

The agent knew from a young age that he would pursue a career in law enforcement. He was a Highway Patrol Explorer Scout at age 14, joined the police department as a dispatcher as soon as he was old enough to legally work, then became a deputy and a certified officer before eventually working as an investigator for the District Attorney. Everyone in Okemah knew Kurt.

When he met the Plackers he officially worked as an investigator for the District Attorney but immediately afterward he went to work for the O.S.B.I.. By September he was assigned to be the case agent in charge. He spent at least three-quarters of his duty time ferreting out clues and suspects in the Weleetka case. He took every criminal incident seriously, but something about the Weleetka murders remained with him at all hours of the day, even off duty. He felt a sense of responsibility to the families, which meant he kept in regular contact, even when he had no good news to report, which was most often the case.

Authorities acknowledged that the sketch released in the first days of the investigation hindered their progress rather than helped. One official stated that two-thirds of the county "has some sort of relation to the Creek tribe" which meant they had to use up precious resources to interview numerous individuals who resembled the sketch. Again, they came up empty-handed.

After eliminating approximately one hundred people from a list of potential suspects and facing a drought of substantial leads, the O.S.B.I. released a dramatic phone call made to 911 on the day of the murders. The recording revealed an unidentified woman's voice whom they later identified as Taylor's grandmother. She screamed, "My God, my God, my baby!"

Officials hoped that the desperate cries might strike a nerve of humanity and motivate someone with a connection to come forward. O.S.B.I. agents alone logged over 10,000 hours by August. Those hours did not include the time invested by the District Attorney, ADA Reilly, the sheriff's deputies and the Oklahoma Highway Patrol. The F.B.I and the U.S. Marshals Service joined in to work the case. Officials working the War Room pulled twelve hour shifts, sometimes sixteen. Much of the work involved extensive database research of license plates and vehicle makes and models associated with the initial O.S.B.I. sketch. They researched every white Chevy pickup truck in the area and then followed up with the identified owners.

Autopsy results made available to the public revealed that the girls had not been sexually traumatized. That detail came as a relief, as ADA Reilly had been plagued with questions about the way Taylor's body had been found, with her legs positioned in what seemed like an unnatural manner. Her legs had been in a diamond configuration, with the feet touching and her knees splayed open.

The autopsy results served to emphasize the question in the prosecutor's mind of why Taylor had been shot in the face while Skyla had not. This detail led to speculation that Taylor's killing appeared to be motivated by anger. That particular shot struck profilers as an indication of some sort of rage rather than a spree killing. The O.S.B.I. began to show signs of frustration, citing a "lack of cooperation" from the public. Investigators interviewed every known violent criminal in the area with no significant outcome.

**W**ith all suspects eliminated and leads rapidly disappearing, the investigative team turned their focus to the most definitive evidence collected from the scene: the gun casings and bullets and therefore, the murder weapon. Agent Green had identified five spent .40 caliber Smith and Wesson shell casings in the roadway beside the bodies. The closest shell was approximately eight feet north of Taylor's body. Green noted that they would have been fired by a .40 caliber-type weapon. The shells were processed in a laboratory in Tahlequah and then a second time in Edmond, Oklahoma. Because the shells were on the ground, Mr. Green surmised a semi-automatic weapon was used, which ejected the shells from the weapon upon firing, as opposed to a revolver.

The five shell casings were sent to O.S.B.I.'s Agent Terrance Higgs, a specialist in projectiles. He assigned each casing an item number and evaluated them under a comparison microscope for markings that would reveal whether or not they had been fired from the same gun. Using this method, Agent Higgs determined that all five of the casings picked up from County Line Road were fired by the same weapon. He determined the weapon had to be either a Glock or a Smith and Wesson Sigma. Another method Higgs employed focused on the drag mark. This mark comes from the firing pin which puts a mark on the casing. The Glock firing pin has an elliptical shaped firing impression, an effect that happens in all Glock pistols.

Higgs also received projectiles removed from the bodies of Skyla and Taylor from the Office of Chief Medical Examiner in Oklahoma. He identified these as copper jacketed .40 Smith and Wesson bullets with rifling on them that was consistent with projectiles fired from a Glock pistol - the same caliber as the casings found at the crime scene. This information appeared to be the only reliable lead into which the investigative team could sink their teeth. The citizens who had responded to the letters identifying registered Glock owners had their weapons tested right outside the county courthouse in a perimeter set up by officials.

Kurt Titsworth and ADA Reilly settled in for the long haul. But neither of them imagined it would take three more years and yet another local murder before the scattered pieces of the Weleetka puzzle would begin to come together.

When she wasn't working long shifts in the war room Maxey made an effort to be present for her recently widowed best friend, Claudia. One of the ways Claudia sought relief from her sorrow was through communication with a spiritual medium. Before Ronnie's death she met with a woman out of Oklahoma City who conducted something called a billett reading. The word 'billett', translated from French, means note or letter. At that time Claudia was seeking connection with her beloved mother. The medium's method was curious. She would gather a roomful of people together and have herself blindfolded by a member of the group. Each person would write down two questions, fold the paper up and place it in a basket. Then the medium would reach in the basket, pull out a folded question and touch it, even rubbing the paper on her face. Then she would begin speaking to the group. On their first meeting Claudia submitted a question about her mother. The medium rubbed the note and began by saying, "I feel a spirit reaching out to me...the spirit is singing, 'I Have the Joy, Joy, Joy, Joy Deep in My Heart'." Joy was the name of Claudia's mother, and the song was one that she had sung many times to her daughter. Claudia became convinced that the medium had a gift.

Still in the throes of grief after Ronnie's death, Claudia decided to seek out the spiritual medium once again to try and make a connection with her lost loved one. A local friend scheduled the billett reading and Claudia asked Maxey to join. Maxey had been very supportive of Claudia in the wake of her husband's loss, but here she drew a line. She was very skeptical of things spiritual, in particular the sketchy world of palm readers and mediums. She declined the invitation. Another friend called to press the issue and Maxey gave in. She sat by Claudia in the middle of the group and the medium began her work. She asked everyone to write their questions and place them in the basket while she had herself blindfolded. Claudia, of course, wished to hear from her husband, so she wrote a question for him. Maxey, exasperated by the whole thing but determined to see her friend through, jotted down this question, "Who killed Skyla and Taylor?" She placed the question in the basket.

The medium began as she had once before and said, "I feel a spirit reaching out to me...for some reason I'm hearing Ronnie Milsap ..." It soon became clear to the group that she was speaking of Claudia's deceased husband. Maxey, taken aback, reached her hand low and grabbed hold of her friend's hand. That's when the medium said, "Ronnie says it's ok, he's happy and he says it is important to maintain the supportive relationship you have right now. He wants you two to keep holding hands." Maxey and Claudia were bewildered but the blindfolded woman was not yet finished.

Maxey was prepared to bolt after the bizarre comments from this strange woman, ostensibly communicating messages from her deceased friend, Ronnie. Then the reading took a different direction and began to address Maxey in particular. The medium began by speaking of a little girl. She said, "there's a young spirit here, a little girl. She says not to be scared for her because she is in heaven with her best friend." The medium told the group that the murderer would be caught. She said when he was arrested he would have curly, red hair, and that law enforcement would bring him to justice using a database. Then the billett reader said, "Wait, Ronnie is back now, he's telling both of you, in a weird, sort of codependent way, you need each other. Keep connected." Maxey left the billett reading still a skeptic at heart, but she was a skeptic with chills running through her body.

# CHAPTER 6

## A Series of Cages

*You never saw it coming*
*No, you never knew how*
*That the poorest and the overrun have overcome you now*
~Killer, Samantha Crain

**A**s all other leads evaporated and a sense of hopelessness took root in the Weleetka area, the O.S.B.I. focused their efforts on the only hard evidence from the crime scene: those bullets and their casings collected from the road and from the girls' bodies.

After community members responded to the dragnet by voluntarily bringing in their guns, Kurt Titsworth was left with approximately twenty gun owners who either had not responded to the request or reported that they no longer owned the Glocks that had once been registered under their names. He set out to track down each one.

Among the handful of owners who contacted the O.S.B.I. to report that they no longer owned their .40 caliber Glock was a local police officer by the name of Woods. He recalled selling his weapon to a young man who worked at the Henryetta McDonald's.

The transactional process of a police officer selling his duty weapon to a civilian for cash in an undocumented exchange may strike the average citizen as most unusual. However, it is not uncommon in the State of Oklahoma. The state has grappled with a budget crisis for decades, despite regular operation within its borders by prosperous oil and gas companies. The monetary mismanagement in state government reached crisis levels at the turn of the century. The state failed to adequately fund even the most basic of governmental services, such as law enforcement and education. In 2007, Oklahoma small town law enforcement agencies could not allow for officer service weapons in their budgets.

The average starting salary for a police officer in Oklahoma is $42,720. That amounts to nearly ten thousand dollars less than the national median annual salary. From that disappointing figure, police officers are expected to provide their own service weapon. In a pinch, a used Glock can fetch up to $400 on the open market. Given the numbers and circumstances it was not such an odd event that Officer Woods would sell his weapon to a civilian.

Although Officer Woods was able to report the transaction to the O.S.B.I., he could not immediately remember the young man's name from the gun sale. His interactions with the purchaser of the Glock had been minimal back on that day in January 2007. The officer usually grabbed his lunch on the go, and the McDonald's in Henryetta was one of the local places he frequented to grab a quick bite. Woods ordered his food and pulled up to the drive-through window. The bespectacled young man with dark hair who worked the fast-food window struck up a friendly conversation with him about firearms. It was not an unusual discussion at all for the area, in fact, shop talk about weapons went on all the time inside the joint. Within two or three interactions the the officer asked the young man if he knew anyone in the market for a Glock. Officer Woods had a Glock to be rid of and he was also in need of some extra cash. There had been no associated paperwork with the sale; documentation of the exchange was required by neither state nor federal regulations. When Officer Woods contacted Agent Titsworth, who was now the lead on the case, to inform him of the missing Glock, the detective took note of the missing weapon. It was just one among a horde of possible rabbit holes to run down.

But after a methodical investigation of every missing Glock, one by one, Titsworth received a call in the autumn of 2009, over a year after the Weleetka shootings. It was Officer Woods. His memory had been jogged about meeting that young civilian. Three months after speaking to the O.S.B.I. about the sale of his Glock, the officer stopped in at the Subway in Henryetta for a sandwich. As soon as he saw the man working behind the counter he knew it was the same fellow who had purchased his gun in 2007. The name he had struggled to provide for so many months suddenly returned to him. The young man with the Glock .40 was Kevin Sweat.

Kevin Sweat had been a figure on the investigation's periphery for months. The connections were there, but like a seedling on a springtime breeze, they floated just out of reach. The young man, in his mid-twenties, struck a slight figure on a 6'0" frame with typically shaggy, dark brown hair and mousy features. He possessed a chameleon-like ability to change his appearance. Some photographs of Kevin depict a chubby-cheeked, curly, red-haired youth, while others capture a dark, rail-thin, gun-toting goth.

His parents, Curtis and Deborah, were married for thirty-five years and from their union three boys were born: Eric, Kevin, and Brian. The children grew up shooting guns. They very much prized the family gun culture. In fact, the men of the family bonded over little else besides firearms. The boys didn't care for hunting deer and duck, like their father. They shared a penchant for the very act of shooting itself. Young Kevin showed an early propensity for weapons that eventually developed into avid enthusiasm. The relationship with his father was often tense and strained. He didn't feel a close bond with his brothers either because of a large age gap.

Kevin was known to be a bit of a loner as a young man in middle school. Teachers recalled that he dressed up as Dick Tracy and sometimes hid in trash cans, like Oscar the Grouch. The only other students he gravitated toward were other social outcasts. Bullies sometimes got the better of Kevin and he was suspended for fighting. But otherwise he maintained a fine record and even received Student of the Year recognition based on his attendance and grades during two years of study at a local technology center. He attended one year of classes at Oklahoma State University in Okmulgee before dropping out.

Kevin had very few friends in school and even fewer afterward. He moved from fast food franchise to fast food franchise, including KFC, McDonald's and Subway. Despite shifting from place to place, he was noted to be a reliable employee. He left for an unsuccessful stint in the military, after which he returned to Okmulgee County to resume his fast food work. He moved back and forth between the towns of Henryetta and Okmulgee for several years. His family, though scattered about after his parents divorced, remained nearby. Kevin spent most of his adult life living with his mother in her well-kempt, cheerful looking home. He also lived with his Aunt Delinda off and on over the years. They maintained a very close relationship, despite Kevin's antisocial personality. They spoke almost every day. Delinda admired Kevin's imaginative nature and his dream of becoming a writer. She regularly allowed him access to her computer so he could concentrate on writing his stories.

Kevin developed a strong online personality during his stays with Aunt Delinda perhaps to compensate for his lackluster social life in reality. He was no exception, since the last two decades have witnessed a phenomenon in which almost every member of society leaves behind an electronic trail. These self-generated profiles do not necessarily amount to an honest reflection of an individual's personal life, but often portray more of an expression of life as we wish to be perceived.

One of the most prolific outputs of Kevin's online personal expression occurred on an artwork-oriented social site. DeviantArt was the 8th largest social community on the web when he began sharing his work there. Kevin used aliases on the site named Giseppie Longfellow, Josepi Morgan and Jacob Conway. The artwork he posted was comprised mostly of personal photography and some original drawings. The photos and sketches were sometimes accompanied by blog commentary. Kevin seemed to enjoy some degree of anonymity within the online community. He received steady feedback and encouragement there. Examples of the images he posted include a baby's pacifier sitting in a pool of blood and a tiny bird held tightly in an imposing fist. Of course, the inclination to post dark imagery and expression of angst is not at all an indicator of a violent disposition. Nonetheless, it is safe to say that Kevin's personal art expression conveyed a rather dismal outlook.

Kevin discussed his desire to become a writer, having drawn and written a cartoon series featuring a character he named 'Johney Darkness'. The comics were extremely violent in nature. DeviantArt acted as his primary conduit for creative and personal expression. He invented another identity for himself named 'Josepi Morgan'. He enjoyed a completely different life online. No longer the shy one or the loner, he was engaged in a social world, albeit a world cloaked in morose undertones. He expressed himself more in online posts than he ever did with family members or coworkers. He stated that very sentiment himself, writing, "try to find something to make me feel more real instead of a ghost who can only be seen on the web".

On DeviantArt he was free to discuss his favorite influences from popular culture. Kevin often cited his favorite music and lyrics, including metal bands such as Mushroomhead. His writings and drawings often reflected a fascination with violence and serial killers, sometimes with satanic themes. Co-workers recalled that he joked in the workplace about shooting and blowing people up. He wore a

Charles Manson t-shirt and became focused on the Green River Killer. Kevin also wrote about cartoon characters he most identified with, like Cheese, a screaming, whining character from Foster's Home for Imaginary Friends, and anime characters like Miroku, a figure who was cursed by a pierced hand that would one day bring about his demise.

Perhaps Kevin's bleak artistic expression should come as no surprise, since great personal tragedy plagued his family. He wrote about a particularly dark period in his life that came after the death of his nephew Landon Jewell. He expressed a strong desire to leave Oklahoma after the thirteen-year-old was shot in the face by the son of a police officer. Kevin became convinced that the O.S.B.I. looked the other way in the boy's death because of the law enforcement connection. Kevin wrote that he believed the boys had been arguing about a girl when his nephew was shot in the head. After it happened, Kevin contacted the press and even claimed in his blog to have done some television interviews on the subject, demanding justice for his nephew. He wrote, "now we're waiting to see if charges will be filed, which there better be…". His complaints were largely ignored, although Kevin would later claim that his public protests made him the target of local police. The juvenile who shot Landon was convicted of first-degree manslaughter and sent to serve out his sentence in a juvenile facility until age eighteen. But Kevin was not satisfied that justice had been done and the angst he had been harboring since his youth continued to build. He continued to express a strong desire to leave Oklahoma and start a new life elsewhere.

Another devastating event befell Kevin ten years prior to the shooting death of his nephew, when his older brother died in a Henryetta motel room from a drug overdose. It was an event that Sweat family members identified as another defining moment. Kevin wrote in his blog that he had *"fucked up alot* [sic] *over the years"* and that if he could go back in time to warn himself he would. He said that when his brother died *"part of me really did die, and I don't like myself..."* These were the reasons, he wrote, that he had to leave Oklahoma, had to change his name, to *"in a way...ok, not actually kill myself, but kill off Josepi."*

He wrote, *"People might think that what I'm doing is extreme, but how far will you go to change? To break away?"* In one of his longer pieces of prose he write this sentiment on his assessment of the human condition:

*"Last year I was at Petsmart, I was looking at the birds, and saw a lone parriot [sic] in a cage. I was just staring at it, and it stared right back at me, and that's when I realized we are all more like birds in a giant series of cages. In our own cage, looking out to the 'outside' world, and into everyone else's cage, expecting each other to do the same thing in our cage: eat, sleep, walking around, fly (if we could). We must allow ourselves to continue this*

*pattern, to be kept as birds in a cage. Whether we live long and 'fulfilling' lives isn't as important as the media makes it out to be, but what matters is that we choose to be free, break from our cages. Fly far...fly high...never be captured again..."*

Kevin bragged online about crushes and interactions with a number of girls, some of whom he mentioned by name. One specific name that never came up was his actual girlfriend, Ashley Taylor. Ashley's and Kevin's paths first intersected in middle school. They were both assigned to an after-school tutoring program for students who were experiencing trouble with attendance and academic performance. Ashley had on the one hand, a bubbly, social personality, but she was also plagued with depression, for which she took medication. Ashley suffered several emotional health concerns in young adulthood. After she and Kevin began dating she sought in-patient care at a mental treatment center in Wagoner, Oklahoma because she had taken too much aspirin.

She was the eldest of three children and a certified member of the Choctaw Nation. She stood a diminutive five feet tall with a heavy build. Her hair was long and blonde. She was by nature a shy person, though not the type to let anyone push her around. She was the kind of girl who would stand her ground if someone tried to hurt her or someone she loved. Both of Ashley's younger siblings were disabled and required special care. She held a very tender place in her heart for them and relished her role as big sister. Patricia and Michael Taylor, Ashley's parents, split when she was just eight years old, but she remained close to both of them. Her mother described their relationship as good and close. They were a very religious family, though various levels of disability kept them from regular church attendance.

Ashley's best friend was a skinny, dark-haired girl with serious eyes, named Anna. Like Kevin and Ashley, Anna suffered through a difficult upbringing. Anna also suffered stinging rejection from fellow classmates because she didn't look like them and she didn't act like them. She began to dress like a goth as an act of defiance, donning all black and chains to show the popular kids that she didn't care to be included in their social circles, anyway. As dark and threatening as they hoped to portray themselves, deep down Ashley and Anna felt much like any other adolescent teens. They were both insecure with themselves and their troubled families, and in search of an accepting place. The three misfits, Kevin, Ashley and Anna, formed an unlikely alliance and gave each other the acceptance each one desired. They delighted in looking up pictures of ghosts and studying the paranormal. Without much parental supervision to guide them, they began to meet up at a local park at night to smoke weed and wander around together. They enjoyed walking the back roads.

The two girls began to spend more and more time together. They had sleepovers and went to church together. The girls shared a passion for the occult and all things supernatural. Ashley confided in Anna that she saw ghosts everywhere, and that they sometimes contacted her to communicate. The ghosts had been visible to her since early childhood, she said, and they were always around.  She claimed to have prophetic dreams. Ashley took up Paganism and Wicca and slept with crystals under her pillow at night, though she continued to go to church and considered herself a Christian. Anna didn't judge her friend crazy, she simply listened to Ashley's bizarre stories and accepted that something, whatever it was, bothered her best friend.

They were drawn in particular to a place called Nichols Park Lake in Henryetta. The quaint location is a city park located two miles south of town, developed in the late 1930s. The main attraction of the park is a small lake, with a couple of docks reaching out over the water. It is surrounded by a steep, tree-lined hillside to the south and several old rock buildings on its northern shore. The biggest of these buildings is known as the bath house. The park is in a secluded location. The official hours available to the public are from sunrise to sunset, but the kids sometimes sneaked in after dark. It was at the Nichols Park bath house that Ashley told her friends she sensed the highest levels of paranormal activity. She claimed to communicate with apparitions she saw there.

Ashley and Anna were boy crazy, and they both had a crush on Kevin. He struck them as a sort of quiet, damaged, artist-rebel boy. Anna was already nurturing a prodigious talent for sketch art and painting. Kevin also drew, though his talent was no match for Anna's. The trio became tight. Kevin even gave Anna a heart-shaped box of chocolates for Valentine's Day. Still, Anna could tell that the real romantic connection existed between Ashley and Kevin. Nothing notable came of their love interest at the time. Ashley did not handle public education well and she dropped out. The three misfits went their separate ways for several years. Kevin went on to graduate and took up a new job working at McDonald's. But Ashley never forgot about Kevin.

Ashley and Anna reunited after high school. Their kinship had not diminished in the least. They began to spend a lot of time together again. Ashley still claimed to see ghosts all around. Anna's brother had died and she struggled daily with the loss of that bond. The two girls decided to experiment with a Ouija board to try and contact him. They didn't have any money so they fashioned the board themselves from pieces of cardboard. Anna was struck by the energy she experienced the first time they tried to communicate with the spirit world. The center of the Ouija board went ice cold. They believed that they contacted Anna's deceased brother. According to Anna, he began spelling out messages. Despite their exhilaration at what seemed like actual contact with the supernatural, Anna's brother delivered a dire message. He told them that another entity was present, but that unlike him, this spirit was bad. It was not human, he told them. Anna's brother told the girls he was scared of the other entity and that he had to leave.

Although they felt frightened, they also felt feverish with excitement. They continued to experiment with the Ouija board. Ashley still had the lanky boy she remembered from middle school on her mind. She asked 'the spirit' she and Anna believed they had contacted to "go fly over to Kevin and tell him to call us".

Fifteen minutes later the phone rang. It was Kevin Sweat. They had not spoken in years. Kevin told Ashley that he had liked her since middle school. That was all it took for the two to rekindle their initial attraction. They immediately began dating. Anna, sensing the connection between her best friend and Kevin, decided to bow out. Unlike their younger days, she now had the feeling that she was a third wheel.

Kevin was physically affectionate with Ashley in front of her mom, always hugging her, brushing her hair and calling her "Sweetie". Patricia Taylor believed from Kevin's actions that he was very much in love with her daughter. While Kevin and Ashley's relationship flourished, Patricia and her daughter maintained a good relationship. They spoke every day, or at least every other day on the phone, if not in person. The two were so close that even after Ashley moved out of her mother's home, it was very unusual for more than two days to pass without speaking on the phone.

According to multiple sources Kevin and Ashley enjoyed smoking marijuana together. They liked watching movies and 'Natural Born Killers' was their favorite. During the wedding scene in the movie the male lead, Mickey, pulled out a knife as he and his beloved Mallory stood on the Rio Grande Gorge Bridge overlooking the water far below. The two lovers cut each other's palms and pushed them together, bleeding, then they threw their belongings over the bridge. The Cowboy Junkies crooned 'If You Were the Woman and I Was the Man' in the background. Ashley and Kevin became obsessed with the film, not necessarily because of its violent themes, according to one friend, but because they fantasized about running away to live a nomadic lifestyle together. The couple dreamed of getting married on a bridge just like the movie. Kevin solemnized their affection by buying a pair of matching rings in the shape of a snake swallowing its own tail.

When Ashley's father, Mike Taylor, learned she was in a relationship he demanded to meet his daughter's new beau. That afternoon Ashley brought Kevin to meet her father and step-mother. Mr. Taylor sat in a chair cleaning his Glock .22 when Kevin entered the room to shake his hand. Any intimidation Mike may have intended to pass on to the new man in his daughter's life was lost as the two men made an instant bond over the firearm. They discussed gun mechanics, shells and silencers. Kevin seemed relaxed and talked about how silencers work. Mike felt satisfied after the meeting and believed his daughter appeared happy.

As the relationship progressed Mike and his wife Faye saw Ashley less and less, although they continued to assist her any time she asked. She called from time to time to borrow money. Her parents were happy to help the young, struggling couple. But with time they both sensed that their daughter had taken on a different personality since she had taken up with this Kevin Sweat. They discussed the issue between themselves but chose to respect Ashley's choices.

Ashley and Kevin lived with Patricia Taylor for about a year. During their stay with Patricia, Kevin worked two jobs at fast food restaurants, first at McDonald's then at Subway. The couple eventually saved up enough money to move into their first place together at the Turning Leaf

Apartments in Okmulgee. Ashley was 23 years old. She told her mother that she didn't want to "live in sin any more," and that decision was, her mother presumed, what prompted the couple's engagement. Ashley stopped by her mother's Okmulgee home to inform her that she and Kevin were going to be married. Ashley had come home wearing a ring, excited to tell her mother that Kevin had asked her to marry him. Kevin proposed at a location that had become familiar to them since those strange days back in middle school: Nichols Park Lake. It was a location that loomed large in their future. Ashley proudly wore the engagement ring Kevin bought for her. It was a modest ring with just one very small diamond on top. She was happy to have a promise of faithfulness from her amor at last.

The second time Ashley and Kevin came together, there was a new urgency and a darker energy associated with their connection. They enjoyed making Molotov cocktails and tossing them out in the field for fun. Shooting guns was also a favorite pastime. Conflict began to rear its head. Kevin continued to see other women and Ashley discovered his infidelities. She became jealous of other women in Kevin's life, including his beloved Aunt Delinda. Ashley and Aunt Delinda met for the first time in December 2010 at the funeral for

Kevin's young nephew Landon. Delinda recalled that the situation in which she first met Ashley was very negative. Ashley approached Delinda at the funeral demanding to know who Delinda was, stating, "well, i'm his fiancee."

Delinda replied, "well, it's news to me, this is not the place to discuss it. We'll talk about it later."

When Kevin visited his aunt's home Ashley usually refused to go inside. She preferred to wait in the car, even during the heat of the summer.

The rekindled bond between Kevin and Ashley also took a toll on Ashley's friendship with Anna. The couple had turned down a dark path in Anna's estimation, much darker than the experimental period of their youths. Ashley no longer wanted to leave her apartment. It seemed that Kevin had taken to sheltering Ashley away from everyone around them. Ashley had regularly contacted Anna to bring them weed and Anna often obliged. She usually went to the couple's apartment and hung out with Ashley while Kevin was away at work. They talked and smoked together. Sometimes they would get out of the cramped apartment to drive through at Kevin's workplace and razz him in the drive-thru window. Anna noted that the couple's apartment was in awful shape, with rubbish everywhere. In the midst of the filth, Ashley and Kevin kept two rats in a cage. Ashley also kept a black cat called Stormy.

Ashley told Anna more strange stories about the energy between she and Kevin. She said they had been fighting much more of late and that sometimes at the height of their arguments, inanimate objects would begin to fly around the room. She said that during one such incident a knife flew off the counter and stuck in the wall. The tension between the couple continued to escalate, until one day Ashley called and asked for weed. When Anna arrived Kevin met her out at the car to pick up the smoke. They no longer wanted Anna inside the apartment. Anna got the distinct feeling that night that the Kevin she had known and crushed on before was no longer there. She was hurt by the rejection from the very friends who knew exactly how painful that sort of rejection felt. She was bothered that Ashley didn't feel free enough to take up for their friendship, or to get out of the apartment anymore. Ashley didn't even seem to have enough ambition to get a driver's license. But Anna knew that Ashley was crazy about Kevin and that, above all else, she wanted to stay with him. She sensed that Ashley would always give Kevin the benefit of the doubt because she loved him so much. Ashley was not willing to give up on that connection for anything, including Anna's loyal friendship. Anna was due to head off for college around that time and she accepted that her best friend had made up her mind. So Anna decided to walk away from the situation, though she never stopped loving her friend.

After an emotional roller coaster couple of years and much romantic insecurity, Ashley called her stepmother Faye on July 5, 2011 to announce that she and Kevin would soon elope. The girl was ecstatic during the call. She had been hoping for a real commitment from Kevin for a couple of years. But later that day when they all met in person, Faye noticed Ashley's mood had changed and that she "was pensive and in fear. Completely closed off the moment her fiance came over to greet me."

Her sudden change of heart was not the only hint that something was amiss. Kevin's blogs, where he expressed his innermost thoughts, never contained a word about the couple's prospective marriage during the same time frame. He wrote instead about his plans to leave Oklahoma for good. He wrote with affection about other women but never Ashley. He mirrored his angst to at least one other person, an old acquaintance who ran across Kevin at Subway. There, Kevin opened up about leaving for good and selling off his things for traveling money. He also had unkind words about Ashley, explaining that she made him feel trapped and that although he tried to break off the relationship, she would not let him go.

Kevin likewise failed to mention his engagement plans to his own family. His mother had been aware that her son and Ashley were an item for three years, but he never mentioned an engagement. He did however express his dissatisfaction with the relationship from time to time. On occasion he remarked about plans to break things off. He told his mother that Ashley had threatened to spread lies about him if he broke up with her, but he failed to specify just what kind of lies.

Sometime after the nephew's funeral Delinda became aware that Kevin and Ashley were living together. Kevin confided more in his aunt than anyone else about the relationship, and according to what he told her, he had no desire to marry Ashley whatsoever. In fact, he told Delinda he wanted to leave Oklahoma and begin a new life. He never told his aunt that he loved Ashley. Sometime in the spring of 2011 Kevin repeatedly began to express his desire to break off the relationship and move away. He specifically said he did not intend to take Ashley with him and that he was working on plans to end the relationship. Delinda actively discussed Kevin's plans for breaking away. They brainstormed about the places he could go when he left. They practiced the things he might say to Ashley on the day before the wedding, when he planned to give her the news that they would not, in fact, be getting married. During the time they discussed these prospective plans, Kevin began bringing quite a few of his personal belongings over to his aunt's house. He stored boxes of them there. He reasoned that he wanted a place where he could easily pick up his things when it was time to go. Delinda understood from their planning sessions that Kevin planned to break things off with Ashley on July 17th, 2011, just as they were supposed to leave to be married in Louisiana.

## CHAPTER 7

# Sissy Is Going To Be Home

*I'd set ablaze the secrets we concealed.*
~Hang Me in the Tulsa County Stars, John Moreland

Agent Kurt Titsworth's first face-to-face encounter with Kevin Sweat came in January 2010, when the detective met with him for an interview associated with the sale of the missing Glock reported by Officer Woods. The interview took place in a Walmart parking lot in Okmulgee. Sweat freely admitted then that he had purchased the Glock from Officer Woods. Kevin told Kurt that he sold the gun in April or May of 2007 to a girl he identified as Meagan. He said Meagan worked at the Henryetta KFC, but could not recall her last name. He told the investigator that he thought Meagan must have moved away, and that he had neither seen nor heard from her since 2007. At that time, the agent was continuing to investigate the missing registered Glocks from the area, and the one reported by Officer Woods was only one of several that had not yet been accounted for.

Without any solid proof to identify that particular Glock as the one used at the Weleetka crime scene, Kevin was free to go.

That first encounter with Kurt Titswirth was not Kevin's first incident with law enforcement in recent history. The Oklahoma Highway Patrol had contacted Curtis Sweat just that previous autumn to retrieve his son's vehicle. Kevin and Ashley had been involved in a traffic stop wherein he was arrested and charged with misdemeanor possession of marijuana. Ashley was released. The trooper discovered an empty Glock box during a search of the vehicle. The Glock box was empty, and in the recording Kevin can be heard saying to the trooper, "I bet you're wondering about that Glock box." But the trooper dismissed his comment and continued to search. After the officer was out of earshot and Kevin was in custody in the back of the patrol car, he could be heard remarking to himself, "This is funny."

When Curtis arrived to retrieve the car he also took possession of the weapons that had been confiscated as a result of the search. Among them he found a cache of guns, swords and ammunition inside. Kevin was transporting a 1911.45 pistol, a .223 rifle, a small shotgun and a .454.

The number of guns Curtis retrieved that day came as no surprise whatsoever. He had raised his sons around firearms and taught them how to properly maintain and care for them. He took the weapons and stored them away until his son was released from custody. The two rarely ever spoke on the phone, but once a week or so Curtis popped in to Subway to check on his son. Curtis had a house under construction at his wooded property just outside of Weleetka. He didn't live full time in the new place because there was no running water yet. He had a girlfriend in Henryetta and stayed at her place most nights. But he did run out to the Weleetka place and check on things just about every day.

Kevin spent some of his free time each week out at his father's Weleetka property. He preferred to go there alone. As he got older he had even fewer friends than in high school. Kevin went out to the secluded area to hang out, shoot his guns and wander through the woods.

Curtis was aware of Ashley but his son never spoke much about her. In a rare moment of candor, Kevin spoke to his dad about his life with Ashley at Turning Leaf apartments. He seemed satisfied with their relationship as best Curtis could tell. Kevin never mentioned either a possible marriage or an impending breakup to his Dad. He also never asked for a loan to finance a wedding trip to Louisiana, as Ashley had told her mother.

Kevin told his Aunt Delinda that he was going out to his father's place on the day before he and Ashley were due to leave for Louisiana. He had settled on a plan. He told his aunt that he planned to tell Ashley that he was going to his father's house to pick up the wedding loan and that he would drop her off at her mother's, telling her that he would come back to get her later. Then, he said, he would just not go back. That was his plan to get free from the woman he had asked to marry him, according to his aunt. She spoke with Kevin about his plans once more on July 17th, the fateful day when Ashley had told her family she was due to leave for Louisiana to be married.

The last time Patricia Taylor saw her daughter was July 15th, 2011. The day came only a few months after the engagement. Ashley told her mother of their plans to marry in Louisiana. Patricia took her daughter to get her hair cut for the wedding. Ashley told Patricia that Kevin's mother had procured a one bedroom rent house for the couple to move into upon their return. Kevin had said that he would borrow four thousand dollars from his father for the trip.

Patricia recalled that just before the two left for Louisiana, Ashley brought all her things over and said Kevin was taking his things to his aunt's and that he would bring other items belonging to Ashley over that night. Patricia thought it strange that Kevin would only bring Ashley's things and none of his to store there, but she recalled that Ashley seemed happy that night. She told her mother that they would leave two days later, on July 17th. Their plans, as Ashley relayed them, were to be gone for two weeks and return on July

29th. Ashley's cell phone had been shut off three or four months before they left, but Ashley promised her mother that she would call from her fiance's phone after their Louisiana nuptials.

But Patricia never received another call from her daughter. She remembered that Ashley took with her a little ice chest and a blue duffel bag when she left. Kevin came back by her house on the 15th, late at night, to borrow her son's portable DVD player because, he had said, Ashley wanted to watch movies on the ride to Louisiana. When Patricia last saw her daughter she was wearing that little engagement ring, her prescription glasses, and she had her wallet that she used to carry her I.D. and medications.

Since Kevin and Ashley were now sharing a phone, Patricia tried calling on the 17th. She wasn't too alarmed when she couldn't reach them. She assumed the couple were enjoying their honeymoon in Louisiana. But she became terribly alarmed when Ashley's brother had a birthday on the 24th of July and still no call came. Ashley would have called him, Patricia felt certain, because he was disabled and she had always been there for his birthday. She knew that Ashley would not have skipped calling, not even for the honeymoon. Patricia started having a strange feeling then, but she squelched it, hoping that perhaps the two newlyweds were just out having fun celebrating their marriage.

When her daughter didn't show up as she had promised on July 29th, Patricia Taylor knew something was terribly wrong. Ashley's little sister kept staring out the window repeating, "Sissy is going to be home."

But she never made it. Patricia called her sister. Together they went over to Kevin's mother's home in Henryetta. When they talked to Kevin's family, however, they found that no one there was aware of the couple's plans to marry at all. They learned that at the same time Ashley told her mother the couple were leaving to get married, Kevin was telling his family that the two had broken up. According to Ashley's family the people at the Sweat home were "acting really strange".

After that, Ashley's family went to Turning Leaf Apartments in Okmulgee, where Kevin and Ashley lived. Kevin was not there at the time but they asked a man who also lived in the apartments to call if he spotted Kevin. Several concerned members of Ashley's family were gathered at Patricia Taylor's home that evening when the phone rang at approximately 11 p.m. Kevin had been spotted at the apartment. The family rushed over to the apartment and blocked in Kevin's car so that he could not escape.

Kevin sat unresponsive in his car. Ashley's mom screamed at Kevin, "you better not have done anything to my daughter!"

But Kevin did not respond.

Ashley's family returned home and phoned the police department. The police responded immediately and Patricia Taylor filed a missing person report for her daughter.

Kevin went to his aunt's home and told her that he and Ashley had gotten into an argument while driving. He said that after the argument became volatile, he stopped the car and she got out by the roadside. He claimed that the last time he saw her, she was walking in the direction of her mother's home on Highway 75. Delinda noted that as Kevin relayed the story he acted nervous. He didn't make as much eye contact as usual.

Kevin asked his aunt if she'd be willing to talk to him alone for a moment. She agreed, and when they were alone he asked if she would still love him if he had done something really bad. His aunt reassured him that yes, of course, she would still love him. But Kevin still was not satisfied. He continued on with his line of indirect questioning and asked if she would tell on him or if she would lie for him. Delinda answered no, that she would not lie in any case. She asked Kevin to explain the reason for which he might ask her to lie. But after that question Kevin shrugged off further inquiry and told his aunt it was no big deal.

Delinda noted several curious traits about her nephew's physical appearance that day, the day after Ashley's disappearance. Besides his unusual behavior, avoiding eye contact, seeming withdrawn, she said she noticed that he was very hot and sweaty. Kevin appeared to be sunburned. He asked to take a shower. He had to go to work at Subway that day. After he got ready he put on his uniform and left to go make sandwiches.

The next day Delinda saw Kevin again and her curiosity was still piqued from their strange interaction from the day before. She began to ask more questions. She wanted to know what had happened with Ashley. She asked Kevin how Ashley had taken the news that he wanted to break up with her. Kevin replied, "Not very well." He explained that Ashley became explosive at the news that they would not be getting married. He said she began yelling. Delinda and Kevin spoke about Ashley frequently after that and he told her a consistent story to explain Ashley's disappearance. He maintained that she had exited his car and began walking toward her mother's house. It wasn't until later that he told a much different story.


Ashley's family refused to accept Kevin's explanation. Mike Taylor directly confronted Kevin about his daughter's disappearance and Kevin replied, "I suppose I'm going to get blamed for this, just like the Weleetka girls."

Mike was taken aback by the unprovoked statement. It was the first time anyone had spoken of a connection between Kevin and the Weleetka murders, so far as the Taylor family knew. Patricia was shocked by the possibility that Kevin might have inflicted harm on her daughter. Over the course of their relationship, she had never sensed that Ashley was afraid of Kevin, and likewise never felt that he might be given to violence.

Around the same time that Ashley's mother tried to reach her on the 17th, Curtis Sweat found something very curious at his Weleetka home. There was evidence of a small fire out back. Curtis had not been there the night before, so he headed out that Sunday around 5:00 p.m. To his knowledge, no one was supposed to stop by the place in his absence. But it was clear to Curtis someone had been by that day. About twenty five yards to the north of the house he found evidence of a fire, the charred material measured approximately five feet in diameter; ash and soot. There he found a styrofoam cup with the initials KS written on the side. In fact, there were two cups sitting by the foundation of the house, about twenty feet from the fire, but only one of them bore his son's initials written on the top.

Curtis was alarmed to find that the unattended fire was still smoldering and he hurried to extinguish it with water. Frustrated that his son would compromise the property in such a reckless manner, Curtis took the lid off the cup that had

Kevin's initials on it and used a drill bit to tack the lid on the side of the house. He wanted his son to see the lid and know he was not pleased. A burn ban had been in place at the time and Oklahoma wildfires regularly flared up with just a hint of wind in such conditions. He called his son to express his dissatisfaction. Kevin explained to his father that he had simply gone over to roast marshmallows and wieners the previous night. He also mentioned that he cleaned out his car and burned some trash.

Curtis allowed the event to pass, but on July 18 he returned home to find that the fire had rekindled. It appeared to him that the fire had been rearranged and put back into a small pile, as though the embers had been stacked back up. Curtis kept old containers around outside the house to collect rainwater. He typically used them to water his house plants. This time they came in handy to once again extinguish the fire on the north side of his house. It looked to Curtis as though someone had changed the form of the fire.

He attempted to contact his son a second time, but by the 18th he found that Kevin had changed his telephone number. Curtis called over to speak with Kevin at his mother's house. Kevin admitted to his father that he had indeed been back out to the house, but that he had only gone out there again to check on things. Curtis told his son he better not be burning over at the property any more, at least not until the burn ban was off.

When Curtis poured water on the fire he used his boot to kick around the embers. A dark glint of something in the ashes caught his eye. He reached over and pulled a shiny object out of the burnpile. It was a ring. He mentioned the curious find to his son. Kevin explained that the ring must have accidentally been swept out with some of the stuff he burned from his car on the 17th. Curtis examined the piece of jewelry carefully. It was a ring with one very small diamond on top. He tossed it back down on the ground.

The Chief of Police at the Okmulgee Police Department contacted Kurt Titsworth to investigate Ashley Taylor's disappearance. The agent spoke with Kevin at his mother's home on August 2, 2011, one week after he had been questioned by Okmulgee police. The questioning quickly turned to Ashley. Kevin mentioned that he had considered breaking up with her. He told the agent that he and Ashley had an argument in the Fall of 2009, during which she called him a bastard and brought up the Weleetka murders. Kevin told Titsworth that Ashley had told him then that she would find a way to get Kevin in trouble over the case if he ever tried to break up with her.

Kevin explained to the investigator that he wanted to get married, but then again he didn't want to marry Ashley because of her anxiety, as he described it. Kevin blamed Ashley's mental health concerns for the problems in their relationship. He told Agent Titsworth that when he left on the morning of July 17th that they left together, with Kevin giving her the impression that he wanted to be married, but his actual plan was to break up. According to Kevin, the two left in the car in the early hours and headed toward Henryetta from Okmulgee. By Kevin's account he set the alarm clock for them to get up that morning to go to his father's house and see if he would loan them the money, and that was what they were en route to do when they got into an argument in the car. Kevin said he let Ashley out beside the road. Then he claimed to drive out to Nichols Park where he stayed until around noon. Shortly after that he drove to his father's place in Weleetka where he set a fire to roast some marshmallows and burn some tapes and manuscripts.

Kevin volunteered to take Agent Titsworth on a little drive to recreate the day. First, they headed south on Highway 75 to Henryetta and turned west on Main Street, which would have taken them right past the McDonald's where Kevin had purchased his Glock from the police officer some four years prior. Then they turned south and visited Nichols Park Lake, then took a back road toward Weleetka. As they wound around the countryside, Agent Titsworth was struck by the realization that the road they were driving, which Kevin claimed to drive regularly from Henryetta, led not only to the homes of Kevin's grandparents, his father's home and his brother's grave site, but also to the location of the 2008 shootings. Kevin made a comment to the detective that he "could feel some sort of force on the road." Afterward, Kevin took Agent Titsworth to his father's property, where they found the gate locked.

When pressed, Kevin advised investigators that if they wanted to find Ashley's whereabouts, they should contact her best friend Anna. But by that time Anna hadn't spoken to Ashley for months. When the O.S.B.I. called to inform her of the disappearance, Anna didn't take it seriously. She thought of the times when Ashley had feigned illness for attention. Her feelings were still hurt over the way her friend had so easily dismissed their friendship after so many years. Anna brushed the call off and imagined that the whole fiasco was probably just a prank. Perhaps her friend had stayed up late partying and gone loopy. Maybe Ashley had finally taken off on that road trip she always dreamed about, Anna thought.

# CHAPTER 8

## Answers In Ashes

*I am fearful I confess*
*How am I to get my rest*
*The house I built is burning.*
~The Housefire, Evan Felker

Lyndon Spears, an officer working for the Okmulgee Police Department for two years at the time, was on duty July 29th. He received a dispatch call about a possible missing person. When he responded he was met in the driveway by Patricia Taylor, who explained to him that her daughter was supposed to have been in Louisiana to get married and was due back on the 29th, but she hadn't returned. When Officer Spears was unable to contact Kevin by phone, he sent a dispatch to Henryetta Police Department, who sent officers out to Kevin's mother's house.

Kevin then contacted the police department and Officer Spears spoke to him by phone. He told the officer that he would voluntarily come to the police station for questioning. Officer Spears waited but Kevin did not show up in ten minutes, as promised. The officer later learned that this was because when Kevin tried to leave the apartment complex he was stopped by the large group of Ashley's family. Officers escorted Kevin from the parking lot to the police station where he waived his rights and sat down to talk about Ashley's disappearance.

Mike Taylor had also joined the search for his daughter. He called Kevin's cell phone but it had been disconnected and so had Ashley's. A contingent of near twenty family members and friends joined the search to find her after he learned she was missing. They arrived at the apartment complex where Kevin and Ashley lived around midnight on July 30th. There, they discovered Kevin attempting to leave. The family surrounded Kevin with their vehicles. Mike walked up to confront Kevin. "Where is my daughter?" he demanded.

Kevin replied once again, "I suppose I'm going to get blamed for this like I did the two Weleetka girls."

Mike, a physically imposing man, told Kevin he knew he had killed Skyla and Taylor and now his daughter. He told Kevin he was going to contact the O.S.B.I. Then Kevin began to beg for Mike to just go ahead and kill him.

Mike entered Kevin and Ashley's apartment. What he found inside was a chaotic mess, with clothes scattered throughout the place and an open suitcase partially stuffed with Ashley's belongings. Her backpack was there too, with her prescription medication inside. Then behind the bedroom door he found a sealed container of something that looked very much like human ashes to him. Mr. Taylor did not collect the bag, nor did he touch anything else in the house, as he recognized it was most likely a crime scene.

Faye, his wife, called the Okmulgee Police Department to inform them of the things Mike saw inside the apartment. Officers arrived, but according to the Taylors, they declined to enter the apartment at that time.

Disgusted that the apartment was not immediately secured for crime scene processing, Mike contacted the O.S.B.I. to report that their missing daughter was likely connected to the Weleetka murders. The Taylor family began to look into Kevin's online activity, where they discovered his plans to leave and a timeline to do so, which corresponded with the timing of Ashley's disappearance. Three months prior Kevin wrote of some vague plans on his online journal on the DeviantArt site. In an April 14th entry he wrote, "Ok, more shit has happened since my last entry, as title claims, I have about 3 months to get my stuff payed

[sic] off and get what I need and leave oklahoma once and for all." Kevin went on to write about his murdered nephew and then returns to the topic of Ashley. "Anyway, back to me, I got in touch with one of my friends that I haven't spoken to since a bad confrontation between her and my 'fiance'..." The date of his plan is titled, "3 months to go . . ." He made his plan public three months and three days before Ashley disappeared. He posted the song, 'Embrace the Ending' to accompany his writing.

Mike began to recall his many conversations with Kevin over past few years. He remembered after the 2008 murders when the O.S.B.I. sent out its letter to all .40 caliber Glock .22 gun owners. Mike had later asked Kevin if he received a letter but Kevin said no, he didn't get one because he claimed that his was a 9mm. Mike completely forgot about that discussion until the night he confronted Kevin about his daughter's disappearance. He asked him directly, "So what did you do with your gun?" Kevin responded, "What gun, my Glock .40?"

Two Okmulgee officers did eventually return to enter the apartment to conduct a welfare check and make sure Ashley was not harmed inside. The officers arrived at the scene and a neighbor informed them that he had only seen Kevin coming and going from the apartment in the last few weeks. Ashley's family waited outside and urgently expressed concern for her safety. When the apartment complex manager arrived his key would not open the apartment door. The officers began searching around the building and found a south bathroom window open. When they looked inside they saw that hot water was running in the bath tub even though no one appeared to be home.

One of the officers climbed through the bathroom window and unlocked the front door. Upon entering they found the place in a horrendous state. According to the officer it appeared as if the place had not been cleaned in months. Grime and dirt covered everything. The officers noted a very curious detail: the bottom of the tub was scrubbed spotless, but the remainder of the bathroom was disgusting. There was a half-packed piece of luggage in the bedroom. Bugs were visible on almost every visible surface. There was a new bottle of bleach and some rubber gloves in the floor.

Upon returning to the police station the officer secured Kevin's consent to search his car. The officer recalled that the car was comparable in condition to the apartment; very messy. In the front of the car the search turned up miscellaneous knives, machetes and tools. He found an empty handgun magazine in the front console. Then the officer searched the glove compartment and found Ashley's wallet, containing her I.D., debit cards, and a C.D.I.B. card. Upon opening the trunk, the officers found a large chopping axe with a red handle and a black head. The axe was three and a half to four feet long. The officers noted some type of substance on the axe that they thought could possibly be identified as blood droplets. It was entered into evidence.

Kevin told Officer Spears a story that corroborated the version he had already told before. Once again he claimed to have been on his way to borrow money from his father for the marriage when an argument began between the two of them. He said that Ashley became irate and shouted vulgarities at him, then demanded to be let out of the car. This time, though, he added a detail that she even tried to get out of the car before it had come to a full stop. Even after she got out, Kevin claimed, the two continued shouting at each other until she slammed the door and he drove away. He claimed that the last time he saw his girlfriend was in the rearview mirror as she walked south on Highway 75. Kevin voluntarily provided a Buccal D.N.A. swab, his fingerprints, and a written consent to search his apartment and vehicle. At the interview's conclusion Kevin was allowed to leave.

When the O.S.B.I. returned to search his apartment the next day officers noted that many of the items that had been there during the initial welfare check were now gone. Faye Taylor drove out to the apartment several weeks later to document the contents of the apartment with her camera. When she arrived she discovered that the apartment had been remodeled, and everything Mike Taylor reported seeing inside was now gone.

Officer Spears entered the apartment one last time that week, in order to assist the O.S.B.I. as they performed a Luminol test to detect any traces of blood in the apartment. The Luminol test did not reveal any blood evidence but Spears noted that a lot of things had been moved out in the time that had elapsed since he first did the welfare check inside.

The next day Agent Titsworth accompanied Agent Real to the interview in which Kevin began to change the substance of his story. First, he claimed that the car door hit Ashley on the head and caused her to fall on her knees beside the road as he drove away. Then he asserted a story that as the couple drove, she started yelling, saying that she knew he didn't want to marry her and that she wanted to die. So, he claimed, he had driven her out to Nichols Park Lake where she grabbed a knife and cut herself. Eventually he recounted a third version, wherein Kevin himself had cut her after she cut herself. He went into great detail as he told the story, claiming that he looked into her eyes when she fell onto the pier, and then he had pushed her into the lake. To augment his horrific account of Ashley's fate, Kevin added more details that he told Ashley, "I love you," repeatedly as he killed her and that he could tell from the look in her eyes that this was what she wanted, and that he had wanted to join her.

In the cross examination of Agent Real the defense team again focused on the failure of Kevin Sweat to have been properly advised about his Miranda rights prior to his lengthy interviews with O.S.B.I. detectives. Kevin said he wanted to die several times. The defense attorney implied that Kevin had cried throughout the interview but Agent Real corrected him: "I never saw a tear."

After the lake story Agent Titsworth, along with divers and other investigators with O.S.B.I. searched the Nichols Lake area for evidence that would support Kevin's version of what happened to Ashley. They were unable to find any evidence to corroborate Kevin's account.

When asked if they had ever broken up before, Kevin once again mentioned an occasion in 2009 when the two had gotten into an argument and Ashley told him that she was going to tell that he had something to do with the Taylor Placker and Skyla Whitaker homicides.

Curtis Sweat took the little charred engagement ring to Agent Titsworth after he learned that Kevin had become a suspect in Ashley's disappearance. This was the first time the detective found out about the fire on Curtis Sweat's property. When he learned that Kevin had burned something in that location, Agent Titsworth executed a search warrant on the Weleetka place. They began searching on Friday, August 5th. The agent drove through the gate on the south side of the property, which the elder Sweat always kept locked otherwise. They proceeded up an inclined driveway to the property set up high on a wooded hill. At the top of the drive a modest, brown house sat in a clearing. The burnpile was still apparent, even several weeks after the fire had been set. It was located about twenty-five feet north of the house, that is, on the back side of the house; the opposite side from the main road that passed by to the south.

Curtis told the agents that Kevin regularly enjoyed shooting guns on the property. He specifically identified Kevin's favored shooting area on the east side, near the railroad ties. The investigative team focused their search in that area. Within minutes their metal detector picked up on numerous spent shell casings concealed from obvious sight by dirt and leaves. Among them, O.S.B.I. agents located nine .40 caliber shell casings and submitted them for analysis at the forensics center in Edmond.

After the thorough search of Curtis Sweat's property concluded, Agent Titsworth contacted Ashley's family to inform them of the devastating news that many of them already suspected. Inside the burn pile the investigators found several pieces of severely fragmented bone as well as a pair of eyeglass frames. Agent Titsworth matched the burnt eyeglasses to pictures he had seen of Ashley and found them consistent with the style she wore.

In addition, the agent found small bra clasps and Just My Size buttons, a kind made special for ladies' wear. Just north of the burn pile the agent located a piece of broken eyeglass lens and a .45 shell casing. He also found a number of other shell casings twenty or so feet from the burn pile, scattered around the backside of the house.

The remains they recovered from the burn pile included muscle tissue, a hand bone, an arm bone, vertebrae, a hip bone, leg and foot bone, knee bone, plus skull and teeth fragments. The recovered bones amounted to 20% of a normal human skeleton. Their condition after being charred in the fire meant they could not immediately be identified by D.N.A. analysis as belonging to Ashley Taylor. The most the investigative team could say at that time was that the bones belonged to a female and that they were consistent with Ashley Taylor. The O.S.B.I. informed the Taylor family that further forensics testing would have to be done for confirmation, but they were 98% sure the charred remnants belonged to Ashley Taylor.

Armed with hard evidence that linked Kevin as the prime suspect in Ashley's murder, Agent Titsworth launched an investigative flurry. He obtained a warrant to search Deborah Sweat's home. There, he found .40 caliber Smith and Wesson ammunition - the same type and brand as the bullets recovered from the bodies of Taylor and Skyla. He also found .22LR caliber bullets in the home. Titsworth next went to work searching

Kevin's brother, Eric's home, where he located a Glock .40 gun box. The serial number on the box was EKG463US but there was no matching gun to be found.

Agent Titsworth gained a colleague from the F.B.I. just a few months after the homicides in Weleetka. Mark Knoll played a key role in chasing down multiple out-of-state leads over the next several years. Titsworth requested that Agent Knoll conduct a firearms trace in a national database maintained by the Bureau of Alcohol, Tobacco and Firearms. The database was designed to trace a firearm by its unique serial number to its original maker and first seller. To the agent's simultaneous shock and relief, the database returned an extraordinary account of EKG463US's life. It would prove to be the most crucial break in the case to that point.

**A** few weeks later, still believing her best friend had simply gone off on a road trip, Anna logged on to Facebook and scrolled through to find Mike Taylor's page on her newsfeed. Anna hurriedly went to his page, hoping to find good news that her missing childhood friend had finally made it back home. Her eyes opened wide as she read what Ashley's father had to say. Mike explained to concerned family and friends who had been following the case and praying for Ashley's safe return that some of her remains had been found in ashes. He wrote that investigators had confirmed she was gone. Anna felt herself go numb as she read the words. She worried that something must be wrong with her emotional state, since she wasn't able to sob or become hysterical at the news that she would never have a chance to reconcile with her estranged best friend. She felt some sort of mental switch flip and her world view took a sudden turn toward the surreal. She could not bring herself to accept that from now on she was no longer Ashley Taylor's best friend. Rather, she had become the best friend of a murdered woman.

## Chapter 9

# A Day in the Life of EKG463US

*That night by the fire his debt was paid*
*When you live by the sword you must die by the blade*
~Caesar the Crow, Buffalo Rogers

EKG463US made its way to the United
States from across the ocean and followed a most
unlikely journey until its arrival at County Line Road
on June 8, 2008. The weapon first entered the
United States during another particularly grievous
time: September 2001. Life for EKG463US began
in an Austrian factory. It was born a Glock .40
model 22, manufactured with thirty-three
components and a polymer frame. Glocks are
imported from Austria into the United States
through the corporate office in Smyrna, Georgia.
Glock maintains corporate records of firearms
received and shipped out of the Smyrna location.
Their documentation satisfies requirements made

on the manufacturer by the Bureau of Alcohol, Tobacco, Firearms and Explosives.

Manufacturers are required to maintain a record of firearm serial numbers for at least twenty years. Glock maintains a log to satisfy this requirement known as the Federal Firearms Log. One man curates these records for the company. The chief method for identifying a particular weapon is by its serial number, located on the frame of the gun. The Glock that was used to shoot Skyla Whitaker and Taylor Placker was identified by its unique serial number EKG463US. The very next month after its stateside arrival, EKG463US made its way north to the Baltimore Police Department. A bailiff for the state of Maryland reported that once the BPD received the new Glock it would have been put through test firing procedures before being issued out to an officer. During the testing procedure the gun was fired in an indoor range and the spent shell casing recovered. The casing was then placed in an envelope, marked with the gun's serial number and sealed. The BPD records show that they conducted the testing procedure on EKG463US on January 16, 2002. Each marking is unique to the particular gun from which it is fired. The police department maintains meticulous records in order to document that fact.

After five years Glock reacquired the gun from the Baltimore PD through a trade-in program the manufacturer has with many law enforcement agencies across the country. Through this program, agencies may opt to trade in weapons for upgrades to newer pistols or to change calibers.

Glock rebuilt EKG463US and sold it in 2006 to Camfour, a corporation out of Westfield, Massachusetts. That was the last transaction to which Glock had direct contact with the weapon. It is important to note here that Glocks are quite distinct from other firearms. When a Glock is shipped out it is accompanied by a gun case which is also marked by the identical serial number and model number of the gun.

In June of 2006 Jerry Robert Bryan of Jerry's Guns Unlimited in Okemah, Oklahoma received EKG463US from Camfour. The gun was in stock for less than one day before it was purchased by a local man named Smokey Patchin. Despite a name that may indicate a citizen less than dedicated to the rule of law, Smokey was actually employed as Chief Deputy for the Okmulgee County Sheriff's office. He followed gun laws to the letter and maintained the required Form 4473, which is generated in the legal purchase of firearms from a Federal Firearms License holder, such as a gun shop, for the purpose of background checks. Jerry's Guns confirmed that at the time the Glock was transferred to Smokey Patchin on June 3rd, 2006, it was delivered along with its case, night sights and three magazines.

Smokey Patchin is a character just as interesting as his name. He is a family man and a familiar figure in Okmulgee County, having served the community with the Sheriff's office since 2003. He kept the gun for little more than six months before he decided to trade it for a different firearm with a Reserve Deputy in the same office. Patchin needed a gun more suitable for shooting competitions, so he traded the Glock 22 for a Glock 35. Smokey traded with Reserve Deputy Jamie Kennedy around October 2006. Again, Mr. Patchin followed the law, in that, there is no legal requirement for documenting the sale or trade of guns among private citizens. When Smokey transferred EKG463US to Officer Kennedy he also gave him a 9mm barrel that Patchin himself had fashioned for the gun.

Reserve Deputy Kennedy kept EKG463US for about six months when he sold it to another law enforcement officer for $350.00 This transaction also included the case, the .40 caliber barrel and the 9mm barrel. Again, this transaction occurred lawfully and without documentation. During that time Kennedy had been working as a Weleetka police officer and had used EKG463US as his service weapon since the city did not have the budget to provide its officers with pistols. Kennedy never discharged EKG463US. This time, when the Glock went to its latest owner, Officer Woods, the 9mm barrel did not go with him.

Mr. Woods was a police officer in the city of Henryetta. He purchased EKG463US and kept it for a few weeks before he found himself in a dire financial situation. As we now know, he struck up a conversation about firearms with a civilian. During the course of their casual acquaintance, Officer Woods asked the young man if he knew anyone interested in purchasing a Glock model 22. The two agreed on a deal and met several days later at the purchaser's mother's house in Henryetta. The transaction was made with cash. At the time of the transfer the gun was once again delivered along with its matching case and three magazines. It is neither unusual nor illegal for private gun collectors to trade firearms without documentation. So it was for EKG463US.


     Firearm identification is a branch of forensic science with an emphasis on determining if a projectile or cartridge casing was fired from a particular weapon. One aspect of this involves something called tool marking identification. This process looks at marks made on a space-specific item and links those marks back to a specific tool. Casings sit at the base of the primer inside the weapon. When a firing pin impacts upon the primer, that's the initiate of the cartridge. The powder inside burns and when the pressure becomes great enough the bullet is pushed down range. The bullet then picks up the microscopic imperfections of the manufacturing process.

Four different elements go on in the manufacturing of a barrel. Steel is drilled out almost to the desired diameter, then they push a rifling tool down into the steel and it is reamed or polished. All these processes add unique features and individuality to a gun barrel. Hence, no two barrels will mark identical because the manufacturing tool is changed each time it is used.

When bullet casings are marked by the barrel, the casing slams against the breech face of the firearm and is marked by that impact. Regardless of whether the casing is made of nickel or brass, the breech face of the firearm is made of steel and the casing takes on the negative impression of the steel breech face. A comparison microscope is then used to evaluate for any matching striae.

It was this forensics process, employed by the O.S.B.I., that matched the casings found in the road near the girls' bodies to the casings found on the property of Kevin's father and the single shell casing kept all those years by the Baltimore police. The tragic outcome proved a worst case scenario for large police departments like Baltimore's, which as a matter of policy, do not sell guns back to manufacturers and refuse to allow retiring officers to purchase their own service weapons. Many police departments adopt similar policies in order to prevent weapons from ending up in the streets. But EKG463US was an exception. It was shipped back to Glock along with other weapons with defects and firing problems, where it was retooled and sold back into the stream of public commerce, good as new.


The autopsies from the Weleetka case were performed on June 9, the day after the murders. The generated report provided the last official piece of paperwork of a day in the life of EKG463US. The type of death listed in the report was "unusual or unnatural" and it stated that the probable cause of death was "Multiple Gunshot Wounds".

A bullet from EKG463US entered Skyla's right arm, fracturing the bone. Another bullet struck the same arm, penetrating soft tissue. The third bullet entered the top of her left shoulder, piercing her left lung, the esophagus, the pulmonary artery, the right lung and her ribs. Another shot hit her left arm, penetrating soft tissue.

Next, a bullet hit Skyla in the chest, passing through her rib, diaphragm, liver, right lung, esophagus, left lung and back. Then another shot went into her chest, perforating her right kidney, pancreas, spleen and left diaphragm. The seventh bullet hit Skyla in the stomach, liver and right kidney. The examination noted the final bullet struck Skyla in the neck. It penetrated her pharynx. The medical examiner noted that at least four of the gunshot wounds individually would have been fatal.

They recovered two damaged copper bullets of different sizes from her body.

The medical examiner noted marker tattoos on Skyla's abdomen that the girls had drawn on themselves at the sleepover the night before. They used pink, red, green, blue and purple markers to write Taylor's name and to reference a boy Skyla liked, writing, "Zac So Hot You Can Cook On Him".

Skyla was wearing a gray t-shirt that read "CHIEFFDINS" across the front, over a pair of red shorts. On her feet she wore a pair of black slippers. She had pulled her hair back with a pink rubber band for their walk to the creek.

Thirteen shots were taken, all seemingly at random, save for one. Only one of the gunshots left powder burns behind because the weapon had been fired so very close to the victim, within three feet, investigators said. That devastating shot was directed at Taylor. A bullet entered her upper lip, passed through her tongue and into the brain. It was still lodged there when the medical examiner performed the autopsy. The second bullet went through her jawline. It fractured her jaw and the base of her skull. This was the wound that showed gun powder, or as the medical examiner so eloquently described it, "fine powder grain with powder stippling". The next shot entered Taylor's right cheek and exited out the back of her neck.

The shooter hit Taylor in the left groin and the bullet went on to strike her colon, small intestine, her stomach, diaphragm, left lung and spine. One bullet passed through her right hand, as investigators believe she raised it to shield herself from the violent onslaught.

Again, the examiner found a marker-tattoo on the little girl from the night before, this time it was a simple heart on Taylor's chest. She wore a ring on her left hand, a light blue Disney t-shirt and red shorts with a pink, flowered bathing suit tank underneath.

This accounting is the last moment for which we can glimpse a day certain in the life of EKG463US. The Glock has never been recovered. Police offered a reward for the gun, which they suspect may have been sold at a Tulsa gun show, but its final resting place remains unknown.

# CHAPTER 10

## The Prosecution

*Now when I think of you*
*What I wanna do*
*I wanna drive down your road*
*Where nobody goes* ~Oklahoma, Nellie Clay

**K**evin Sweat was arrested with formal charges filed against him in the murder of Ashley Taylor on August 12th, 2011, nearly one month after her death. The State held him for a short period of time at the Okmulgee County jail. He then transferred to Okfuskee County. Due to serious threats from other inmates, officials next moved him to Seminole County jail in Wewoka. Despite the other precautions, authorities placed Kevin in a cell with another inmate charged with murder. That man pummeled Kevin inside their shared cell almost immediately upon arrival. Social constructs are present even among the incarcerated. Accused child predators exist at the bottom of that particular stratum. Officials realized they had no other choice but to place Kevin in solitary confinement for his own protection. Seminole County became his new home for the duration of the pre-trial time period.

The prosecutor filed official murder charges against him for the Weleetka murders on December 11th. Kevin had already been held without bail for the murder of Ashley Taylor since his August arrest. The additional charges came several months after, when the State felt confident that the evidence and forensics gathered during the elapsed time amounted to a fortified prosecutorial case.

He was charged in Okfuskee County District Court with two counts of Murder in the First Degree and two counts of Assault with a Deadly Weapon. Oklahoma law requires the State prove four elements to satisfy a conviction of Murder in the First. Those elements are first, the death of a human; second, the death must be unlawful; third, the death was caused by the defendant; and finally, the death was caused with malice aforethought. The law goes on to explain that malice aforethought means "a deliberate intention to take away the life of a human being...'malice aforethought' does not mean hatred, spite, or ill-will. The deliberate intent to take a human life must be formed before the act and must exist at the time a homicidal act is committed." At trial, each of these elements must be proven beyond a reasonable doubt in order to convict.

The District Attorney announced that the State would seek the death penalty. Maxey felt convicted that if she ever believed that any case warranted the death penalty, it was this one. They submitted numerous aggravating circumstances to justify the death designation. The aggravating factor requirement in the prosecution of a death penalty case, according to current law, serves to ensure the ultimate penalty is "reserved for the worst of crimes and is limited in its instances of application." Oklahoma is one of thirty one states in the union wherein the death penalty remains available.

The Eighth Amendment of the Constitution limits capital punishment "to those offenders who commit a narrow category of the most serious crimes and whose extreme culpability makes them the most deserving of execution." Most states require three specific findings before a death penalty sentence may be applied. There must first be a finding of aggravating factors. Aggravating factors in the State of Oklahoma are limited to eight options:

1. A prior felony involving the use or threat of violence;
2. During the commission of the murder, the defendant knowingly

created a great risk of death to more than one person;

3. The person committed the murder for pay or the promise of payment or hired another person to commit the murder for pay or the promise of payment;

4. The murder was especially heinous, atrocious or cruel;

5. The murder was committed for the purpose of avoiding or preventing a lawful arrest or prosecution;

6. The murder was committed by a person while serving a sentence of imprisonment on conviction of a felony;

7. The victim of the murder was a peace officer or correctional employee of an institution under the control of the Department of Corrections, and such person was killed in performance of official duty; or

8. At the present time there exists a probability that the defendant will commit criminal acts of violence that would constitute a continuing threat to society.

Established law also requires a finding of mitigating factors. Mitigating factors include any aspect of a defendant's character or record, and any of the circumstances of the offense that demonstrates a basis for a sentence less than death. The State does not specifically define a list of mitigating factors as it does for aggravating factors, although examples often used in a murder trial include a difficult family history or a history of emotional disturbance.

Finally, the law demands a balancing of both the aggravating and mitigating factors. It is this final balancing requirement that determines the outcome of whether or not the death penalty is appropriate. In other words, the aggravating factors must outweigh the mitigating ones before the State may execute a citizen within the constructs of the Eighth Amendment.

The State of Oklahoma listed three aggravating factors to justify death in its Bill of Particulars against Kevin Sweat:

1.     AS TO TAYLOR PLACKER AND SKYLA WHITAKER: That the murders of Taylor Placker and Skyla Whitaker were especially heinous, atrocious or cruel in the following manner, to-wit:

a.  That the Defendant did incapacitate Taylor Placker and Skyla Whitaker by shooting them and both Placker and Whitaker were conscious, but unable to defend themselves;

b. That Placker and Whitaker's deaths were caused by the defendant shooting them repeatedly;

c. That Placker and Whitaker did feel physical pain and did suffer extreme mental anguish prior to their deaths;

d. That Placker and Whitaker were children, unarmed and posed no threat to the Defendant.

2. AS TO TAYLOR PLACKER AND SKYLA WHITAKER: That the defendant knowingly created a great risk of death to more than one person, to-wit:

a. That the Defendant did incapacitate Taylor Placker and Skyla Whitaker by shooting them and Taylor Placker and Skyla Whitaker were unable to defend themselves;

b. That Placker's injuries were caused by the defendant shooting her repeatedly, in the same manner as he caused the death of Skyla Whitaker;

c. That the victim, Taylor Placker, did suffer the same fate as Skyla Whitaker.

3. AS TO TAYLOR PLACKER AND SKYLA WHITAKER: That there is an existence of a probability that the defendant would commit criminal acts of violence that would constitute a continuing threat to society, to-wit:

a. That the defendant's crimes are violent and his speech and actions during the crime show his callousness and total disregard for human life;

b.  That the defendant's actions after the murder show no remorse;

c.  That the defendant's actions show a pattern of escalating criminal activity and disregard for the laws and rules of society.

d.  There is additional evidence detailing the defendant's participation in other unrelated crimes showing his violent criminal behavior.

If convicted, Kevin's defense team would be tasked with establishing the evidence of mitigating factors to try and avoid the death penalty in sentencing. Kevin's defense attorneys were assigned to him by the Oklahoma Indigent Defense System (O.I.D.S.). The process of assigning a legal defense from O.I.D.S. is initiated by a district court judge who, after reviewing the defendant's financial status, makes a determination that the defendant is unable to acquire representation on his own. O.I.D.S. was created by statute in the 1990s, designed to provide trial, appellate, and post-conviction criminal defense services at state expense.

The court named Wayne Woodyard to the team. He was a seasoned defense lawyer who specialized in death penalty cases. At the time he was assigned to defend Kevin, Woodyard had been practicing criminal law in Oklahoma for over thirty years. He had, at one time, also served as a prosecutor. Peter Astor, another member of the

O.I.D.S system, was the next attorney to join the team. Astor graduated from OU College of Law just seven years prior to Prosecutor Reilly, so he was the more youthful advocate for the defense. Gretchen Mosley completed the trio. She was a tenacious spitfire in her own right, a bellicose woman who did not hesitate to lock horns with the prosecution and sometimes even presiding judges. Kevin's defense attorneys argued that the best way to defend him would be to conduct a single trial before one jury, in one location, with one sentencing. The judge granted that request.

After a defendant is arrested and formally charged with a crime, one of the first steps in the judicial process is the process called "discovery". Perhaps the most crucial phase of preparing for trial is the discovery phase, during which both sides of the criminal case are required to exchange evidentiary findings. Kevin's defense team first filed a discovery motion in December 2012. The discovery exchange can be a lengthy process, as in this case, which included the burgeoning O.S.B.I. report, a monster of a document at approximately seventeen thousand pages. It was the largest amount of discovery in O.S.B.I. history at the time.

Maxey Reilly, as the prosecutor, acted as a sort of gatekeeper of discovery. In criminal cases the prosecutor bears the burden to ensure that all evidence in the State's possession or which can be reasonably obtained is turned over to the defense or made available for inspection. This includes all law enforcement reports and witness statements. Reilly worked with Kurt and others to ensure that everything was turned over to the defense. The open sharing of information is so crucial to the process that a prosecutor is subject to sanctions and even disbarment for failing to comply with the discovery requirement.

Due to the incredible volume of information in the Kevin Sweat case, Reilly and Titsworth devised a method to log every piece of information turned over to the defense. Defense counsel had to sign for every item the prosecution shared and then they were given a receipt. Discovery was an ongoing process leading up to trial, so as any new information became available, the prosecutor was obligated to make opposing counsel aware.

The preliminary hearing was originally set for July, but both the defense and the prosecution requested continuances because of the overwhelming amount of information that had to be dissected. Maxey was stymied by the amount of discovery generated by the case. She was forced to set up a separate, private office at her husband's funeral home for the Sweat trial. There she could be isolated and focus all her energy on the case at hand. The District Attorney's office itself was too hectic, with multiple demands that pulled her in opposite directions, always away from the rigorous study of trial preparation. The funeral home was the one place where she could be certain the people inside would not want anything from her. One homicide was work enough, but three separate homicides in one trial was something else entirely. Both the defense team and the prosecution were tasked with enormous responsibility.

    **A** preliminary hearing is an evidentiary hearing in which the state has the burden of proving that probable cause exists in order to bind a defendant over for trial. The state's burden is to prove that a crime was committed and that the defendant probably committed it. Kevin Sweat had a right to a preliminary hearing, but he also had a right to waive it. The defendant was also able to have two different judges in the case: one to preside over the preliminary hearing and a separate judge for the subsequent trial, if any. Judge David Martin was assigned to preside over Kevin's preliminary hearing.

    Kevin and his defense team decided to take the preliminary hearing option. It served as a strategic decision to allow the defense to see first hand what the State might present as evidence at trial, as well as how potential witnesses would perform under oath. Reilly and Titsworth continued to work closely in preparation for the preliminary hearing. Maxey already knew Kurt from his work in the District Attorney's office, but as they diligently prepared shoulder to shoulder, they became even closer. Maxey noted that he paid extreme attention to detail and worked the case on a personal level. Sometimes when Maxey grew weary and needed a break, Kurt kept right on plowing through. They both worked long hours away from family. The two remained in constant touch, calling each other at home in the middle of the night should a new, random thought on the investigation strike.

The process was not always easy and at times the two colleagues reached points of consternation about how to approach the hearing. Their dynamic became something like that of a brother and sister, with squabbles erupting sometimes late at night if the two differed on a particular strategy. When it came down to the hearing and trial presentation though, the final call was on Maxey.

With trial approaching, she found herself more and more isolated, thinking about how to lay things out. She considered the best way to present the witnesses in an order that would paint a clear picture for the preliminary judge, and ultimately the jury, as to what happened to Skyla, Ashley and Taylor. She wanted judge and jury to know more than just who the victims were, what happened to them and who was responsible. She also felt compelled to convey the actual pain felt by the girls, their families, friends and community. Her skill in the courtroom lay in her ability to convey that sense of grief. Maxey knew that some attorneys were smarter, certainly more experienced. But when it came to making a persuasive, emotional appeal in that courtroom, she had full confidence in her own ability. Just like in high school, she had often been underestimated by other attorneys. By now though, she had learned to use that to her advantage. She sensed that the community where she intended to raise her family depended on her. Maxey considered herself a soldier of sorts and now she prepared for battle.

Defendants exercise the right to a preliminary hearing in the majority of cases wherein significant prison time is at stake. The process allows the defense to have a glimpse of how the State will lay their case out at trial. The flip side of that is, prosecutors often employ the tactic of presenting just enough evidence to meet their statutory burden of proof at this stage in an effort to avoid fully revealing their hand to opposing counsel. It is a strategic waltz, and Maxey, having prosecuted a few lesser trials by this time, understood that part of the strategy. Part of her job was to know just how close she could keep her cards to the vest.

Part of the preparation meant that Reilly and Titsworth met with all the witnesses associated with the case. This included witnesses whom the prosecution knew were hostile to the case. That part of the process can be highly emotional and difficult. Maxey met with Kevin's mother, Deborah, in her office. She was faced with the task of saying to the woman's face that she believed her son had murdered three people. It was a tense meeting but

Maxey plowed through the questions and testimony she intended to use at trial.


The proceedings began on January 28th, 2013 in Okfuskee District Court. Judge Martin brought the court in session and welcomed all parties to Okemah. He asked the parties to announce their appearance by and through counsel, starting with the prosecution.

"Maxey Reilly for the state of Oklahoma," came the prosecutor's reply.

"Wayne Woodyard and Peter Astor with the defendant. We are present and ready, Your Honor," the defense team answered.

The first witness to be called was perhaps the most emotional. As soon as Maxey announced to the court that Peter Placker would take the stand, the defense invoked the Rule of Sequestration, a motion that if granted, orders witnesses to be excluded from hearing the testimony of the other witnesses. The judge granted the request but allowed Agent Titsworth to be excluded from the rule. He was allowed to hear all the testimony but all other witnesses remained outside until it was their turn to testify.

While some of the other victim's family members had expressed their anger during the proceedings, Peter Placker's countenance was one of pure, distilled anguish. The judge gently addressed him prior to his testimony. Peter had never testified before. His body language suggested a man drained of joy. The prospect of asking this man to recount the story of finding his daughter in the ditch was an excruciating one, but it had to be done. The judge assured him that if he needed a recess at any time it would be granted.

The questioning began easy enough. Maxey established how the Placker family came to live on County Line Road and which family members lived in the house. She had to ask for the microphone to be turned up because the man's answers were delivered in a barely audible tone. He remembered how Taylor often walked the fields around their home, how she loved to fish and play with animals. When it came time to recount the events of that awful day, his speech halted from time to time, as if he became short of breath. The pauses helped the man maintain his composure as he once again told a group of mostly strangers about the worst day of his life.

Next, Mr. Woodyard approached Peter to inquire about how many times he had spoken to investigators about the case. He asked if officers had provided any names of persons they thought may be responsible. Peter remembered that a few names had been mentioned as suspects in the first few months. They discussed the items that were taken from the Placker home as possible evidence, including the computer, a rifle, some of Taylor's clothing and a comforter. Woodyard wanted to know about the circumstances of the house burning after the murders but Peter explained that the family moved out of the house before the fire, and that he had no idea what happened. "I don't hardly even go down there," he explained.

Woodyard focused his attention on some of the Placker family members with criminal history.

The attorney asked, "do any of your immediate family members have any felony convictions?"

'Probably a few of them do,' Peter replied.

"Okay. Did they have any history with any people that caused them some concern for their safety or their family's safety in the past?"

'To my knowledge, no.'

The strategy of the defense centered on introducing doubt about the murderer's identity, the precise weapon that can be used to sink even the sturdiest of prosecutions. Woodyard pointed out that two boys on a red four-wheeler had been spotted that day. Peter could not confirm that assertion because, he explained, he'd never seen them.

The discussion turned to Taylor's dogs. Peter told the court that she had eight or nine and that most of them were puppies. He explained that most of them followed the girls to the bridge that day. His account was confirmed by Chase and Douglas Whitmire. They had been driving the backroads to go eat at the Pig Out Palace, when they saw the girls walking to bridge with the dogs.

They had to stop their truck in the middle of the road to keep from hitting one of the puppies as the girls walked by. When the girls and dogs were safely past the men drove on to their supper. Not long after the Whitmire men reached their destination, they noticed the ambulance fly past, lights swirling, siren wailing. Peter explained that by the time he began to walk up to find Taylor and Skyla, most of the puppies had returned back to the house. One of the puppies remained behind and waited in the ditch.

A strategic pattern soon took shape from Prosecutor Reilly's line of questioning. It began with the June 8th murders and ran all the way through to Kevin's arrest, crafting a story for the courtroom as she went. She next questioned Agent Green, establishing his evidence gathering technique at the Weleetka crime scene. They discussed the collection of the spent casings in the road and the chain of custody that followed up until the casings were processed by their ballistics expert. He referred to a Crime Scene Investigation Report during his testimony.

The defense took its turn to cross examine the agent and attempt to poke holes in their crime scene process. Woodyard pointed out that there appeared to be shoe impressions around the cartridge cases in the crime scene photographs.

Woodyard asked, "Your job is to identify what you consider might be evidence or relevant evidence for a particular crime scene; correct?"

'Correct, sir,' the agent replied.

"Okay. Did you take any photographs of what you thought were shoe prints in or around those cartridge cases?"

'Not around those cartridge cases, no, sir, I did not.'

"Okay. So you seem to be a reasonable officer, if you thought someone was standing at or near that location, you would have taken photographs of any shoe prints or boot prints or whatever the case may be that might be related to that. Did you take any photographs?"

'Are you referring specifically to the shell casings area?' The agent asked a question of his own.

"Shell casings only," Woodyard replied.

'I don't recall any shoe impressions around that area.'

The next series of witnesses included six men and set out to establish at great length, how the Glock EKG463US had come to be placed at the Baltimore Police Department, the Weleetka murders, and Curtis Sweat's property.

Maxey sought to establish that the shells recovered from the Weleetka crime scene matched those recovered from Curtis Sweat's property. The O.S.B.I. brought in their ballistics expert, Firearms and Toolmarks Supervisor Terrance Higgs. Higgs received bullets from the Medical Examiner's office. They had removed two .22 caliber long rifle bullets from Taylor and Skyla, but the expert testified they were too mangled to be identified. He explained that when .22 caliber bullets strike something harder than they are, especially when they are made of soft lead, they tend to get beat up. When .22 bullets enter the cranium, they come into contact with dense bone and become mangled. As a result, the two .22 bullets recovered from Skyla and Taylor were mangled beyond the point of identification.

When it came to the other ballistics associated with the case, however, he was able to identify the .40 Smith and Wesson casings submitted by Agent Titsworth. These were the casings collected from the home of Kevin Sweat's father. Higgs concluded that the casings recovered from Curtis Sweat's property were fired from the same weapon as the one that fired and left shells behind at the crime scene where Taylor and Skyla had been murdered. Higgs then retrieved the single casing from the Baltimore police department and compared that casing to the ones collected from the Sweat property, as well as the casings from the site of the murders on County Line Road. He concluded that all the shell casings matched as having been fired from the same weapon.

Agent Higgs stated that of the eleven total casings from the three different sites, he was 100%

certain all eleven had been used in the same firearm. In one of the very few moments of levity in the preliminary proceeding, Higgs explained that ballistics experts tell a joke in cases like this one. He told the court, "they say that Stevie Wonder could identify evidence" such as the kind gathered in the case of Skyla and Taylor's murder. The casings simply matched up so well.

The next step was to prove through Curtis Sweat that Kevin had used his property to fire EKG463US. Curtis confirmed that there were two or three different places where Kevin liked to shoot for target practice prior to 2008. He described an area that a friend had set up using cross ties on the east side of the place about two hundred yards inside the property line. Prosecutor Reilly wanted to narrow down the number of people who may have left behind spent casings on that particular area of the property.

"Do you remember telling Agent Titsworth that Curtis Hammill, Hammill's friend and Kevin, your son, were the only three people that you had seen shoot guns in that specific area?"

'That would be pretty well correct,' Curtis replied.

Deborah Sweat came forward to be questioned after her former husband left the stand. Ms. Sweat denied ever having known that Kevin and Ashley had been engaged, although she did explain that on occasion Kevin made remarks about his dissatisfaction with the relationship. She recalled that he mentioned breaking up with Ashley. Maxey then went to work to establish Kevin's motive for killing Ashley.

"Did your son ever tell you that she had threatened to get him in trouble for the Weleetka murders?" She inquired.

'No," Deborah said.

"Do you not remember talking to Agent Titsworth and telling him that you had had that conversation with your son?"

'He just said that if he broke up with her that she would spread lies about him.'

"And isn't it true that he told you what type of lies?" Maxey pressed the witness.

'No, he did not,' Ms. Sweat said.

The prosecutor did not relent. "So, all he said was that she would spread lies about him?"

The defense team jumped in before Deborah could answer. "Objection, fishing, speculation, relevancy to this hearing," Woodyard injected.

The judge denied the objection, saying, "All right. Given the nature of the relationship, allow her some leeway. Go ahead, please."

The prosecutor dove right back in. "Did you ever tell your husband, Curtis Sweat, that Kevin told you Ashley had threatened to tell people that he killed Taylor Placker and Skyla Whitaker?"

'I really don't remember,' Deborah replied.

"Don't remember," Maxey asked with an animated, inquisitive tone. "Are you taking any kind of medication that affects your memory?"

'Absolutely none.'

"Do you drink heavily?"

'Never, I don't drink at all.'

Maxey then employed a similar approach with Deborah's cousin James McClellan. James had lived with Kevin's mother for some time prior to the Weleetka murders. His testimony, based on previous interviews with Agent Titsworth, could serve to establish that Kevin possessed a Glock after the Weleetka murders, when he claimed to have previously sold it to a coworker. Since the prosecutor still didn't have the murder weapon, his testimony was important.

"How are you today, sir?" The prosecutor asked.

'I'm good,' he said.

"Who are you living with?"

'Debbie Sweat.'

"And what is your relationship to Debbie?"

'She's my cousin.'

"How long have the two of you been living together?"

'Since Spring of '08.'

"Do you ever remember the defendant showing you a .40 caliber Glock handgun that he owned?"

'I vaguely remember a Glock. I don't know the caliber.'

"Do you remember the conversation that you had with Kevin when he showed you that handgun?"

'No.'

"Sometime after Taylor Placker and Skyla Whitaker were killed, do you remember having a conversation with Kevin about the O.S.B.I. questioning him about a gun that was used in those murders?"

'I don't remember the exact words, but it was something in the neighborhood of they questioned me about it and that was about it.'

"And he specifically told you what type of gun they had questioned him about? What type of gun did he tell you at that time?"

'.40 caliber Glock.'

"Do you remember asking him what he had done with the gun?"

'Yes.'

"And what was his response?"

'That he either gave it to or sold it to a woman.'

"Did you ask who that woman was?"

'Meagan, I believe that was the name, was Meagan.'

"Do you remember telling Agent Titsworth that you didn't remember the name of the woman?"

'No, I thought I told him it was Meagan.'

After Kevin's arrest Agent Titsworth subpoenaed records from KFC regarding all employees named Meagan at that particular location. He tracked down both Meagans and confirmed that not only did neither of them buy a gun from him, they claimed to have never even met the man.

The prosecutor then turned to the issue of whether or not Kevin's family had been aware of Ashley and Kevin's engagement.

Maxey: "To your knowledge, was Ashley Taylor Kevin's fiance' or girlfriend?

McClellan: Can you give me a timeframe?

"We'll say in 2011, right prior to her disappearance."

'Well, it would depend on which time you talked to him. One time it was.'

"Was that something that you and Deborah discussed?"

'Probably, yes.'

"So Deborah was aware that he considered her his fiancee?"

'At some time, yes, I'm sure, Yeah.'

"At some point were you aware that Kevin became unsatisfied with his relationship with Ashley?"

'Yes.'

"And did he talk to you about the possibility of breaking up with her?"

'Not in those words.'

"Do you remember Kevin telling you that Ashley had threatened to say things about him if he broke up with her?"

'Yes.'

"What types of things."

'I don't know.'

"Do you remember telling Agent Titsworth that the defendant told you, on two or three separate occasions, he told you that Ashley had threatened to tell people that he killed those girls if he broke up with her?"

'I don't remember telling him that. You'd have to read that back to me.'

"You don't remember that?"

'No, I don't, huh-uh.'

"Are you taking any type of medication at this time that alters your memory?"

'Well - -'

The prosecutor had no further questions for the witness.

# CHAPTER 11

# A System of Men

*And there was static on our radio*
*It cut to the heart, soft and slow*
*Covered us in white noise and snow* ~Elastic HIghway, John
Calvin Abney

Prior to resuming the preliminary hearing on January 29th, Associate District Judge Martin took the unusual step of addressing those present with a bit of an argument in favor of the American judicial system. He first addressed counsel for both the state and Kevin Sweat. He directed them to take a deep breath and relax. The judge then continued with his own grand assessment of the proceedings:

"...*we sometimes forget how great a country we have. We get, we're so involved in the legal system. But it is a great country. We are a system of laws. We are not a system of men. The system we have is why we're here. We all have a role to play. I have a role. The prosecution has a role. The defense lawyers have a role. And it's a great system. If you ever visit other countries, you are ever mindful of the wonderful country we have. And so, just take a moment and relax. Take a deep breath and realize we are part of a great country. We are part of a system where we have in place, the prosecution and defense of people. It's not a third world country. We have safeguards in place and that's what we're doing here. So, that is free. You don't have to, you don't have to take that. You do have to listen to it because I'm the judge, but that's just part of the, part of the perks of being behind the desk here. But we should be ever mindful of the system that we have and be thankful that our forefathers had the foresight to establish a system of laws and the Constitution and the amendments thereof, and so that's a free political science lesson. Free of charge. There's no, absolutely no charge for that. All right. We will resume with the hearing then. So, call your next witness if you would, please."*

Kevin's defense attorney asked the court to address a housekeeping matter. They requested that the defendant's hands be unmanacled so that he would be able to write. Kevin made a habit of taking notes during the pretrial proceedings, which he occasionally shared with the defense team. The judge agreed that the cuffs could come off. It was a decision that would later prove ill-advised. Kevin looked on as his father came under questioning once again, this time by the defense team. They went to work introducing doubt as to whom may have started the fire on Curtis Sweat's property. This time, Peter Astor began by addressing the styrofoam cups found near the fire.

"I think you told Miss Reilly that the fire pit was about twenty-five feet from the house?" Astor began.

'I'd say so , yes,' Curtis Sweat replied.

"The cups that you found, Mr. Sweat, you told Miss Reilly that they were not descriptive of any particular place, Subway or McDonald's?"

'No.'

"Were they styrofoam? Like the cup I have here. Bigger than this though? That's probably six ounces?" Astor gestured toward the beverage that sat at the defense table.

'I say yes, best I can remember.'

Astor began to ask about how many people had access to the Weleetka property. He established that Kevin's older brother Eric had a key to the gate and the house. The defense sought to introduce doubt to the prosecutor's earlier inquiry of Curtis that established only three people had access to the area where the Glock .40 spent casings were found.

Astor: "Miss Reilly asked you about - - oh, Kevin's friends and whether you had knowledge of who he may have brought out there. What I'm trying to determine is how many people could have had access to your property."

Curtis replied with an answer that lent credibility to the defense team's assertion that anyone could have gone up on his property. 'Just about anybody that would drive up from the east side of the property.'

"Where there was no gate?"

'Yes.'

"And you know, you don't know all of Eric's friends, safe to say?"

'No.'

Astor also gleaned testimony from the witness to indicate that Curtis's sister, Delinda, had a key and access to the property, as well as her son, pointing out once again that Curtis couldn't know all of his friends either. On redirect, Maxey sought to establish once again that Kevin, and no one else, had been the one to set the fire that contained Ashley's remains on the night in question.

Maxey: "Mr. Sweat, before the 17th of July, 2011, you said you got to the house, you saw this burn pile. Had there been a burn pile in that spot before?"

Curtis: 'No.'

"To your knowledge, had there been any burn piles in the vicinity of the home prior to that date?"

'There was a brush pile that I burned on the east side. There was nothing more than logs and some odds and ends that we used to start the fire with.'

"But there were no other fires up close to the home?"

'No.'

"In the area where this burn pile was located?"

'No.'

"Did Kevin ever discuss with you, you possibly loaning him money to get married?"

'No.'

"And we talked a little bit before about any prior conversations that you might have had with Kevin regarding his relationship with Ashley. And you indicated, I believe, that you didn't really remember discussing that with Kevin, correct?"

'Yes, Ma'am.'

"Do you remember being interviewed by Agent Titsworth of the O.S.B.I?"

'On several times.'

"And during those interviews, do you remember telling him that you discussed with Kevin his relationship with Ashley?"

'No ma'am, I don't remember that.'

"Do you remember telling Agent Titsworth that you had heard a rumor that Kevin was going to marry Ashley?"

'Yes.'

"Now you also said earlier that when you talked to Kevin on the 17th and 18th about him starting the fire that you didn't talk to him about Ashley; is that correct?"

'Yes, ma'am.'

"Do you remember telling Agent Titsworth that when you visited with him on the 17th or 18th that he told you he had broken up with Ashley?"

'I don't recall that.'

"You also said earlier, I believe, that you found the ring in the burnpile on the 17th or 18th, I think is what you said?"

'Yes, ma'am.'

"Is that correct? Do you remember telling Agent Titsworth that it was actually on the 2nd or 3rd of August before you actually found the ring?"

'No ma'am.'

"Are you certain on what date you actually found the ring? Could it have been on the 2nd or 3rd?"

'It could have been.'

"Do you think that it possibly it was after Agent Titsworth started questioning you about Kevin and Ashley's whereabouts before you went digging in the fire and found the ring?"

'It could have been.'

Prosecutor Reilly next established that Kevin had lost about twenty pounds since he had gone into state custody. She made a point to confirm with Curtis that the north side of his property, where the burnpile was found, could not be seen from the road that passed by to the south.

Maxey: "You described your closest neighbor was about a half mile away; is that correct?"

Curtis: 'Yes.'

"So if you're standing where the burn pile is located, there's no way that someone driving down a road could see what you're doing?"

'No.'

Peter Astor interjected at this point, "I would object as to speculation."

Judge Martin replied, "Be overruled."

When the defense had a chance to question Agent Titsworth on the issue of the burnpile, they set out to try and impugn the evidence gathered at the burn pile at Curtis Sweat's property.

"Okay. You refer to bone fragments. What description did you give to that? Was I correct in writing down fragmented; is that right?" Woodyard inquired.

Kurt answered, 'Yes, severely burned, severely fragmented bone.'

"When I looked at the photographs they looked almost pulverized to me; would you agree with that description?"

'Some of them, I mean.'

"Okay. And to the best of my knowledge, these bones are what have been identified, you say through the forensic anthropologist as human bones have never been identified as belonging to a particular person; am I correct?"

'Well, the bone itself was consistent with being Ashley Taylor's?'

"But they have never been identified as, in using any kind of science, as being Ashley Taylor's?"

'The actual bone itself?'

"Yes."

'No.'

"Okay. Do you know what this ring was made of, what metal?"

'It appears to be gold, but I don't know.'

"So it could be examined and tested later on?"

'Yes, sir.'

"Okay. And the fact that an eyeglass that might be consistent with that that was worn by Ashley Taylor would not be surprising to be found in that fire if Mr. Sweat was in the process of breaking up, was getting rid of her things and his things and burn that in that fire; would it?"

'Yes.'

The prosecutor had earlier questioned Delinda Morrison, Kevin's beloved aunt with whom he had lived and confided. During the testimony, Maxey had been able to extract information to show that Kevin had discussed his plans to break up with Ashley and leave Oklahoma in the Spring of 2011, about three months before she disappeared. Delinda also testified that at some point Kevin changed the story he told her about Ashley's disappearance. He told her, too, that he and Ashley had a physical altercation at Nichols Park Lake and that he had stabbed her in the stomach. The defense team found Delinda Morrison's testimony damaging to an already challenged defense. They set out to undermine some of the most damning elements of her testimony, but she proved to be a formidable challenge to both the District Attorney and the Defense.

Woodyard: "Okay. Let me start then at the conclusion of your testimony regarding the statement that you say that your nephew, Mr. Sweat, made to you about stabbing Ashley Taylor in the stomach at the lake; do you remember that testimony?"

Delinda: 'That was after I found out she was already burned. I don't know the date.'

"Okay. Stop right there. When did you find out that, as you say, that her body had been burned? When did you find that out?"

'Sir, I don't remember the date.'

"Okay. Now, would you agree with me that you wouldn't have been able to find that out until officers had made their investigation of the scene, of Mr. Sweat's property?"

'The day I found out --'

"Would you agree with that? You could not have found out until they had completed their search?"

'Well, glasses were found, and so I don't know.

"Okay. Can you answer my question?"

'No.'

"Okay. Did you ever have a conversation with Kevin while he was in jail?"

'No.'

"Okay. You realize he was arrested on August the 3rd?"

'Okay.'

"Okay. Do you realize the officers didn't do their first search until August the 5th."

'Sir, I don't know. I talked to my brother about the glasses, not the police.'

"Okay. And so he's in jail when they make their search, how is it you had a conversation with him about this matter if he's in jail and you're not having any conversations with him?"

'Sir, the conversation I had with my nephew concerning that occurred at my own home. I don't remember the date.'

"Okay. So this would have been before you talked to Officer Agent Titsworth; is that correct?"

'You mean confirming it was Ashley do you mean?'

"This alleged conversation that you say you had with Mr. Sweat."

'It was before he was arrested.'

"Took place before you had a chance to talk with Agent Titsworth; am i correct in that?"

'Over this, over the remains?'

"Over what you have just told this court about Mr. --"

'Okay. Kevin was the one that told me, Kevin had not been arrested. I don't remember the exact dates, but all I can say is that I was at my brother's home whenever I talked to him about the glasses. Maybe I'm misunderstanding you.'

"You didn't talk to Agent Titsworth until after Mr. Sweat was arrested; isn't that correct?"

'I'm sorry, I don't know.'

Having failed to make any headway with the witness, the defense team made a motion to exclude Delinda's testimony entirely, calling her credibility into question. Woodyard argued that her testimony should be "held for naught" in the proceeding.

The final witness called to testify spent more time on the stand than any others. Maxey saved him for last by design. She believed that he would be the one to close the lid on all the evidence that came before him. He was the one witness who was just as familiar with the evidence as the prosecutor herself. The witness was Agent Kurt Titsworth. Maxey was aware that the investigator had appeared in numerous Okfuskee trials before. Juries were sometimes difficult to assemble on the sheer basis that just about everyone in the area knew Kurt. He grew up there, went to school in the county, began his career there, took his family to church every Sunday in town. The problem Kurt posed for defense teams was that based on his role in law enforcement and community involvement over the years, the majority of potential jurors believed Kurt's testimony over anything else. In the eyes of most townspeople, Kurt Titsworth was unimpeachable. If he said it was so, then in the minds of the townspeople, it must be so.

At the outset, Maxey set out to establish Agent Titsworth's testimony about Ashley's disappearance when he first met with Kevin at Deborah Sweat's home. The first line of questioning was designed to meet the burden of proof that Ashley was murdered and that Kevin was responsible.

Kurt explained, 'When I got there Kevin Sweat was there along with his mother, and Jim McClellan.'

"What specifically did he tell you about his relationship with Ashley?," Maxey replied.

'At some point in time he would say he wanted to get married, but then again he didn't want to marry her. He was frustrated because of some of the anxiety she had. And that was bothering the relationship.'

"So basically, he was telling you that that was the type of thing that was preventing him from wanting to marry her?"

'Yes.'

"Just her anxiety? Did he say anything else?"

'No.'

"Did he indicate to you that when he left Okmulgee on the morning of the 19th that he actually intended to marry her?"

'Yes, that was his intentions was that he wanted to lead her on to believe that they were going to get married, but in all reality, I think they were just - - he was going to break up with her, this was my understanding.'

"So at that point he admitted to you that he didn't have any intentions of marrying her during that two week period that they were going to go to Louisiana?"

'Well, he went back and forth. At one point he would say well, yeah, I really want to, but then again he would say, well, I'm sorry for leading her on. You know, I shouldn't have led her on to think that we were getting married. So it was almost like he was playing games, I guess you should say.'

"So you say he changed his story four times; is that correct? First he told you that he was driving down the road with her that he let her out of the car. Then it went to they were driving down the road, got into the argument, he opened the door, maybe it hit her and she was down on her knees. And then it went to, they went to Nichols Park but none of that had actually happened, that they went to Nichols Park and got into the argument. And that he throws the knife at her, she cuts herself and falls into the lake. Then it progresses to he throws a knife at her, tells her to kill herself, she starts cutting her throat, and then he basically finishes her off and pushes her into the lake. What did he tell you that he did after that, specifically? Did he tell you that he looked for her or tried to get her out of the water?"

'No, he didn't. He got in his car and left and drove to his father's place.'

"After this interview, did you go to the lake or did anyone to your knowledge go to the area of NIchols Park and the lake and search the area for evidence that would support this version of what happened to Ashley Taylor?"

'Yes, that night I did actually did go out to the lake. There was actually some divers there checking the lake that night.'

"Well, during those two days when you were searching the lake and when the divers were searching the lake, were they able to find any remains or anything consistent with what Kevin Sweat had told you?"

'No.'

"Do you know if they found any blood on the pier that would be, you know, support his version of what happened to Ashley Taylor?"

'No.'

"Was there anything else that was found in the Nichols Park area that would support the version of what happened to Ashley Taylor that Kevin Sweat told you?"

'No.'

"After the area of Nichols Park was searched, did you actually conduct some searches on the property of Pat Sweat in Weleetka, Oklahoma?"

'Yes.'

"When was that done?"

'That was actually on Friday, which would have been August the 5th.'

Another key piece of evidence established in the preliminary hearing concerned cell phone records. Agent Titsworth's relentless tracking of potential evidence led him to review the cell phone records of people associated with the case. He focused on dump records, or large amounts of cellphone data, from the cell towers that overlapped the 2008 crime scene during the time that Ashley and Skyla were shot. The time frame the agent isolated and searched was 4:30 p.m. to 5:30 p.m. in the afternoon of June 8th, 2008. Titsworth was able to identify the specific cell phone numbers active in the area. One of those phones was Taylor's, which activated when her grandfather reached inside her backpack and attempted to dial out for help. Another phone number appeared in the search parameters. That number belonged to Kevin Sweat. It showed Kevin's cell phone moving from the Henryetta-area tower, then to the tower that overlapped the crime scene at the time of the homicides. Kevin attempted to explain that he had gone out to visit his grandparents that day, but when questioned, his grandparents could not recall the visit.

The defense team recognized the cell phone evidence as a threat and set out to attack its evidentiary validity, along with the possibility of D.N.A. found at the scene.

Woodyard: "Okay. What, what D.N.A. did you discover that places him at the scene where these girls were found?"

Titsworth: 'I didn't place any D.N.A. evidence at the scene.'

"Okay. No D.N.A. on the Mountain Dew can?"

'Yes, there was.'

"That was associated with him?"

'No.'

"Okay. I understand about the cartridge cases. Were there any D.N.A. associated with Kevin Sweat removed from the cartridge cases?"

'No.'

"Any fingerprints on the cartridge cases that's been identified with Kevin Sweat?"

'No.'

"Okay. The, you testified about these cell records, cell phone tower dump, is that the term, can you work with that?"

'Yes.'

"Where was the tower or towers that you picked up the information from?"

'This tower was the one that overlapped the crime scene was about three miles northeast of the crime scene. '

"How big a circumference did that tower cover?"

'I'm not sure.'

"Okay. It ran in a three hundred and sixty degree circle; am I correct?"

'That's correct.'

"Okay. In this made up story, and I keep using his term, it was made up, that he told you, he indicated that he was driving south on this road; do you remember that?"

'Yes.'

"And isn't it true that if he took off in his vehicle heading south, he would have run right by

Peter Placker's property and the Plackers coming this direction; isn't that true?"

'If he would have continued that direction, yes.'

"Okay. And he didn't tell you that he went any other direction; did he?"

'I believe he said he turned around and went back home.'

"And would you agree with me that throughout this story every time you asked about a .22 he told you he only had a .22 rifle; correct?"

'Yes, he said he had a .22, yes.'

".22 rifle, pistol, excuse me, rifle, not a pistol."

'He mentioned he had a .22 rifle, yes.'

"Okay. And you actually, did you confiscate that rifle?"

'Yes.'

"Okay. Was that rifle tested?"

'I don't recall if that rifle was sent to the lab or not.'

"Okay. But as far as you know, that rifle has not been associated with anything that occurred in this case, has it?"

'No, sir.'


The defense now turned to a delicate topic that would amount to the most troubling evidence in the murders of the little girls. The defense counsel made sure to once again identify Agent Titsworth as the "Case Agent", which specifically meant he was responsible for gathering or at least knowing about all of the evidence or potential evidence that has been covered in the case, including any DNA evidence in question.

Woodyard: "Okay. Have you been provided and have you reviewed some DNA findings by your laboratory?"
Titsworth: 'Yes.'
"And specifically, DNA findings for the items that were taken from the Plackers, like a comforter?"
'Yes.'
"And it's my understanding that the clothing these girls were wearing were recovered from the medical examiner's office and retained by your office; isn't that true?"
'Yes.'
"Now, I'm not a scientist and maybe you can help me with this. Sperm and semen are products of the male gender; isn't that true?"
'Yes.'
"Is that your understanding? And okay, and what I've read is that there were some sperm fractions recovered from the panties of both these girls; do you recall reading that?"
'Yes.'
"Okay."
'But I don't know that it was from both of the girls.'

"I mean on panties of both the girls; you don't recall that?"

'No, sir.'

"You do recall at least panties of one of the girls?"

'Yes.'

"Okay, did that pique your interest, as an investigator in this case, to determine how that could have happened or where, who donated that sperm?"

'Yes, when it first originated, it did. And then after some time, if I can explain, we knew that both the girls shared panties, wore each other's panties, and that there was a lot of - - they wore them for quite some time. And I don't know that that profile was a full profile that was found in one of the panties, but I know that it was a partial, and it was a nasty mixture.'

"And Kevin Sweat was excluded as a donor for any of the mixture contained in that DNA sample, isn't that true?"

'Yes, he was.'

This piece of unexplained DNA evidence appeared to be the strongest argument for the defense to show that another unidentified person had motive to kill the girls, but A.D.A. Reilly went after that suggestion with her trademark tenacity.

Maxey: "Agent Titsworth, I just have a few questions. Are you aware of what sleeping arrangements were in the Placker household?"

Agent: 'I remember somewhat what the arrangements were. I know that it was a small house and that each other, you know, I'm not sure that maybe they had two beds, but I know each other shared each other's beds and - -'

"And Linda Placker and Jennifer Johnson both stayed in the house sometimes as well; did they not?"

'Yes.'

"And did they have boyfriends that stayed in the home with them?"

'Yes.'

"And Charles Placker and his wife slept in the home together at certain times; is that correct?"

'Yes.'

"And the girls both slept in the beds where all of these people slept; is that true?"

'Yes.'

"And Mr. Woodyard was talking about the fact that there was sperm faction found on one of the panties of the girls; is that an accurate statement to your knowledge?"

'Yes.'

"Was there actually sperm found in the panties of the girls?"

'I believe in one of them there was. I think that there was, but I don't know that they were, it was just such a nasty profile that they thought that it was contaminated, or that it was a, you know, being the fact that they changed or they wore their panties for quite some time, and they changed, you know, so, but i believe so, yes.'

"And he asked you if Kevin Sweat was actually excluded as being a potential donor to that mixture; is that true?"

'Yes.'

"Was there anything, did Kevin Sweat ever tell you that he touched the girls while he was at the crime scene?"

'No.'


The discussion hearkened back to some of the most difficult moments for the families after the little girls were lost. The families themselves had come under suspicion for a short time after the murders, when the investigative team still didn't have a suspect. The authorities cleared the families early on, but small town whispers would not relent. A distant second to the pain of their children having been murdered, was the horror of being accused for the act. One of the most poignant moments of the entire preliminary hearing came from the testimony of Linda Placker, Taylor's older sister. A chilling fact established in the investigation was the fact that Kevin worked with both Skyla's mother at the time of the Weleetka murders and later with Linda at Subway. Linda described their relationship as work acquaintances. She recalled in her testimony that Kevin asked specific questions about her sister's death in her words, "quite a bit". He specifically asked her if she knew what the girls had been wearing the day of the murders. Linda noted his curiosity, but at the time it was two years after the girls were shot, and people from the community approached her with questions about it every day.

On the cross-examination, Peter Astor inquired about the day of the murder and then asked Linda, "Now, it is safe to assume that obviously it was a great tragedy to your family, and certainly you are all grief stricken."

Linda replied, "I can't say it was, because it still is."

## Chapter 12

## Pieces Left To Be Found

*It was all burnt and broken*
*Like pieces left to be found*
*But to everything there is a season*
*The reaper don't listen to reason*
*I'da crawled in there with you if I could*
~About Time, Tequila Kim Reynolds

The question of Kevin's mental state became an inevitable point of contention in pre-trial proceedings. The defense employed a number of doctors to gather evidence of incompetence or to find information that could prove to be a mitigating factor should Kevin be convicted. Psychiatrist Dr. Musick examined Kevin and found that while he appeared to be a normal human being on the outside, he had in fact, "accumulated a lifetime of pain, humiliation and anger over a succession of traumatic experiences which socially programmed him to run and hide." Dr. Gary Jones found that Kevin had "Asperger's Disorder which could explain some of his unusual behaviors. Forensic psychologist Dr. Benjamin Frumkin reported that Sweat had Schizotypal Personality Disorder.

A competency hearing went on for several hours in which the line of questioning centered on whether or not he had Asperger's syndrome or autism. The judge, irked at the amount of time these proceedings required, accused defense attorney Gretchen Mosley of "plowing up the same field multiple times, each time with a different tool". The defense team wanted to submit evidence that Kevin suffered from autism but he refused to allow it as mitigating evidence. The debate that ensued amounted to a prolonged episode of dueling psychologists.

Frumkin testified that he conducted a series of tests to determine if Kevin was capable of knowingly and intelligently waiving his Miranda rights during the 2011 interviews. The doctor found that Kevin was not capable. He said that that tests revealed Kevin demonstrated problems with perception and processing of information such that "things get jumbled up in his brain," and that officers may have read his rights too quickly for Kevin to understand. The defense team argued that Kevin may have assumed that because he signed an application requesting an attorney from the Oklahoma Indigent Defense System, that he would have an attorney present in the September 2011 questioning with O.S.B.I. agents. Frumkin wrote that Sweat "misperceives and mis-processes things happening around him." He used an example of

Kevin alleging that officers had poisoned his soda as one example.

The State's expert witness, Dr. Shawn Roberson testified in contradiction of the evaluations presented by Dr. Frumpkins and Dr. Jones. Dr. Roberson reported that Sweat's answers were shifty and evasive, citing his inconsistent responses throughout all of the experts' testing. He further argued that Sweat's testing scores did not meet the criteria for a positive Asperger's diagnosis and that Dr. Frumpkin's conclusions were based on unsubstantiated assumptions. Roberson testified that he found "no signs of severe mental illness, significant mood disorder, or any intellectual disability. Sweat gave contradictory answers on a battery of psychological tests that examined personality traits and understanding of Miranda rights." The physician found in his clinical interactions with Kevin that he declined to answer "very basic" questions about his personality, causing the doctor to conclude that "he didn't want me to know a lot about him".

Defense attorney Woodyard pointed to possible mental issues to call the confession interview into question. He began his questioning of Agent Titsworth by pointing out that Kevin had a good work record at his job in Henryetta at the Subway restaurant. He stressed that the detectives had no trouble contacting Kevin and talking with him about the case. They found him to be cooperative. They began to focus on the August

3rd interview, when Agent Titsworth confronted Kevin with his findings.

Woodyard: "Okay. Now would I be accurate in stating that as you listen to his statement on August the 3rd, both you and Agent Real, neither of you really believed a lot of what he was telling you; am I correct with that?"

Agent Titsworth: 'That's correct.'

"Okay. And did he appear, at least from my viewing of the statement, to be distraught throughout a lot of that tape; would you agree or disagree with that observation?"

'There was a few times that he would act like he was crying. Now, whether it was sincere or not, I don't think so.'

"Okay. But he put his head down on the desk several times?"

'There was a few times, yes.'

"Okay. Made comments to you like, 'I want to die.' Made comments like that?"

'Yes, sir.'

"Okay. Even asked you once, maybe twice, if he was crazy or if he was going crazy; did he not?"

'May have, yes sir.'

"Okay. And in the face of these comments, I mean he makes some other things like, 'I want to go home,' didn't he tell you that?"

'I don't recall that, but he very well may have.'

"Okay. Didn't he also say he wanted psychiatric help or therapy?"

'He may have mentioned something, yes.'

"Okay. On a couple of occasions, did he not tell you guys, 'I don't know what you want me to say,' Did he not use those words to you?"

'He may have. I just, I don't recall all the specifics of the interview was long and there was a lot of things that was said during the interview that I don't recall.'

"I understand that. He did deny on numerous occasions killing Ashley. He said he did not kill Ashley, made that comment explicitly on a number of occasions?"

'He may have made that statement, yes.'

"Okay. And in the face of that, you and Agent Real persisted in your questioning; correct? Kept telling him, 'We don't believe you, we don't believe you,' and then he would change his story a little bit; would he not?"

'That's correct.'

"Do you think he was changing his story to tell the truth or to accommodate the pressure you guys had inserted on him during the course of this interview?"

'I think he was wanting to tell the truth, but not all the truth.'

"Okay. And do you think you got to that level? I mean he trusted you; did he not?"

'Maybe some sort he did.'

"You said on several occasions in this interview, as I recall, that you guys had bonded like the day before; right?"

'We had.'

"And you wanted him to trust you; correct?"

'Exactly.'

"Okay. So you don't think he was just adding these different pieces to this story just to maybe end this interview? Let you hear what you guys wanted to hear?"

'Again, I think that some of the things that he told us was a lie and I think some of the stuff he told us was the truth.'

"Okay. And eventually at one point at the end of this interview that had been going on for several hours and he was clearly tired; was he not at that point?"

'He may have been.'

"Okay. At the end of this interview then he says, 'Okay I killed her'; right? Would you agree with me, it was towards the end of this interview that he made that comment?"

'It would have been toward the end of the interview, yes. '

"Okay. But then immediately after that, didn't he say, 'I guess that's how it happened, I didn't kill her, I didn't kill her,' didn't he say that to you guys?"

'He made statements like that, yes.'

"And that didn't cause you any concern about how truthful this information was that he just provided you as to what happened to Ashley Taylor?"

'Again, I felt like that Kevin had killed Ashley. But he wasn't telling the truth exactly about what all had happened, about how it happened.'

"Okay. But you all had a statement from him about the details and you, among other officers, attempted to verify that story; correct?"

'That's correct.'

"Okay. There are cameras out at Nichols Park; are there not? And officers obtained those cameras in the course of the investigation of this case, the videotapes, excuse me."

'Yes.'

"And am I correct in stating that neither he, nor Ashley Taylor, nor his vehicle were observed at that location on July the 27th?"

'At that certain location where the cameras were at on that day.'

"Okay. I think at one point in time Agent Real told him that he would be surprised if somebody had seen him and what happened out there; do you remember that statement by Agent Real?"

'He very may well have.'

"Okay. Do you guys have such a witness in this case that observed what occurred out at Nichols Park on this date?"

'No, sir.'

"Okay. The pier was checked by a criminalist using Luminol which would highlight or expose blood on the pier and none was found; am I correct?"

'That's correct.'

"Okay. Is this a trustworthy story?"

'I feel like that some of it is trustworthy, yes, I do.'

"Okay. You have indicated under Direct a couple of reasons why Mr. Sweat said he did not want or could not break up with Ashley. Didn't he also say that he was concerned about the reaction of the Taylor family if he broke up with Ashley? Was that also another reason why he would not break up with her?"

'He had mentioned something like that, yes.'

After the defense team presented its best effort to raise doubt as to the legitimacy of Kevin's confession, Maxey began to redirect Agent Titsworth to answer those doubts.

"Agent Titsworth, do you have any idea how many interviews you've conducted in the course of your career?" She asked.

'Oh, hundreds,' he replied.

"Hundreds. And is it typical for you to go into an interview and to have a defendant automatically tell you everything that happened and tell you the truth about it?"

'Oh, very seldom.'

"What more often than that happens."

'Most of the time what happens is you get some of the truth, but you don't get all of the truth. Very seldom does a person that commits a crime tell you the whole entire truth.'

"And rarely do they come out and just automatically tell you the truth. Isn't it fair to say that generally you have to keep questioning before you get any version of the truth out of them?"

'That's correct.'

"And so, the procedure and the type of questioning that you used in your interrogation of Mr. Sweat, were they any different than the procedures and techniques that you've used in the hundreds of interviews before this particular interview?"

'No.'

"So there was nothing out of the ordinary about this interview?"

'No.'


The defense argued that Kevin's confession taken by Agent Titsworth in September 2011 violated his 5th Amendment right not to be compelled to be a witness against himself. They argued Sweat had invoked his right to counsel and that once that occurred based on established law, the State could not re-initiate a custodial interrogation without counsel being present.

They tried to pin Titsworth down on the issue of whether Kevin was able to knowingly waive his rights considering his psychological issues.

Woodyard: "Agent, you interviewed Mr. Sweat on several occasions prior to your interview of September 13th; isn't that correct?"

Titsworth: 'Yes.'

"And you had an idea what kind of personality and person that he was when you went to interview him on September the 13th; isn't that also true?"

'Yes.'

"Okay. You are aware that he had issues, personality issues, perhaps psychological issues, at the time that you interviewed him; isn't that also correct?"

'Yes.'

"Did you also have training and interrogation in your stint as a investigator for the district attorney's office?"

'Yes, I did.'

"So you were aware that you can kind of put someone in a position, just by the nature and structure of your questions, that would result in whatever they say being incriminating; wouldn't you agree?"

'Well, depends on probably the questions that's asked.'

"Okay. Just use an example, you've probably heard of this. I see you're wearing a wedding ring. And if I ask you to answer yes or no, have you stopped beating your wife, what answer would you give me?"

Maxey interjected at this point to object to the relevance of Woodyard's line of questioning. The assertion seemed designed to rattle the detective but Agent Titsworth maintained his calm demeanor. The judge instructed the defense attorney to make his line of inquiry "a little more artful", and sustained the objection.

Woodyard reigned in his line of questioning and continued.

Woodyard: "You started off this interview by telling Kevin Sweat that you really didn't want to hear that he didn't do it, because you already knew he was responsible, and he was there; correct?"

Titsworth: 'Basically, yes, sir.'

"And you said that over and over and over and over again all throughout the interview; true?"

'That's correct.'

"Okay. And so, there are times you cut him off from responding when he wasn't following that line. He was trying to deviate and tell you basically I don't know; isn't that true?"

'There were some times that I did, did cut him off, yes.'

"Would you agree that he has a weak personality?"

'A weak personality?'

"Weak. Weak."

'No, I wouldn't say that.'

"Would you say that he doesn't have a very strong will when it comes to law enforcement officers and talking with them?"

'I mean I feel like Kevin knows what, you know, what he's doing. I feel like he is a game player. And that he's a manipulator.'

"In fact, you're a manipulator, aren't you?"

Again, Maxey objected to the relevance of the aggressive line of questioning directed at Kurt. The judge instructed the defense attorney to ask questions that would elicit admissible testimony.

Woodyard began once again, "did you manipulate this interview in a direction that you wanted it to go?"

Titsworth: 'I set - - this interview was set up as a confrontation to him, and I addressed him in that interview as the facts that I knew about the case. And there was no doubt in my mind when I went into that interview that he was the person responsible for the one that killed those two little girls on June 8th, 2008, and my mindset was that I wasn't going to let up until he quit or until he asked for an attorney.'

The argument presented by the defense, which argued that Kevin had invoked his right to an attorney in the O.S.B.I. interviews, gave Maxey the opportunity to demonstrate her grasp of settled case law on the issue. She countered that the defense counsel pointed out three separate incidents during which the defendant invoked his Constitutional right to an attorney. The first of those incidents occurred on August 3rd, 2011. During that interview, the defense team argued that Mr. Sweat says toward the end of the interview, "Do I need an attorney?" However, after a pause, the defendant clearly says, "I need an attorney."

Maxey countered by stating she and five others listened closely to the recording and what the defendant actually said was, "Am I going to need, like, what do i need, an attorney?" She went on to cite United States Supreme Court precedent from the case *Davis v. The United States*, wherein the Court ruled, "The statement for counsel must be unambiguous, for if a suspect makes a statement that is ambiguous or equivocal about wanting an attorney, that might be a request for counsel, questioning does not need to end." So, according to established law, a defendant simply asking if he might need an attorney is not the same as definitively telling an officer 'I want an attorney.'

After considering the videotaped statement of Kevin and all arguments for and against allowing the confession as evidence, the court found the taped statements to be admissible and that the continued questioning after Kevin's ambiguous requests for counsel were not violative of the 5th and 6th Amendments.

The defense team continued to argue that the actions of police and state detectives were violative of 4th Amendment. They attacked the first entrance Officer Spears made into Kevin and Ashley's apartment the day she went missing. The officer had referred to his entry as a 'welfare check', since there had been no warrant to enter. Mr. Woodyard pointedly asked the officer on the stand if he had been trained to believe that a welfare check is an exception to the search warrant requirement. Officer Spears replied that he and his fellow officer were not searching for anything that had to do with a crime. He asserted that the two officers entered strictly for the purpose of checking on Ashley's welfare, swept the apartment to make sure no one was inside, and when they observed that no one was, they secured the apartment and left. Woodyard, still not satisfied, questioned what Officer Spears meant by "swept the apartment". Spears replied that it meant quickly looking through various rooms without searching. Kevin's defense counsel, with these methods, skillfully invoked a legal doctrine called "The Fruit of the Poisonous Tree," which is intended to make evidence inadmissible in court if it is derived from evidence that was illegally obtained.

As the preliminary hearing neared its conclusion, Woodyard went for a hail mary, presenting an argument based on Oklahoma precedent which required that the state must present evidence of each element of the offense that they've alleged. Woodyard argued that in the case at hand, the prosecution had failed to present evidence of murder in the first degree, i.e. malice murder, which he described as "basically death of a human, death must be unlawful, must be caused by the defendant, and caused with malice aforethought." The presence of bone fragments on Curtis Sweat's property, he argued, were not identified as belonging to any specific individual. They were identified "in a general sense by, I guess a forensic anthropologist's report that it might be consistent with a female, a young female of a certain age." He argued that the report did not reflect that the D.N.A. established that the bone fragments belonged to Ashley, because the charred remains provided only a partial profile. As such, he concluded, the D.N.A. report should be deemed unreliable.

Woodyard continued to use Ashley's autopsy report as evidence that the state had failed to establish homicide. The medical examiner in the report does write that the "cause of death and the manner of death is uncertain in this case."

He concluded that that medical examiner's report provided no evidentiary value to the court in proving two issues, that the death was unlawful, and that the death was caused by the defendant.

His argument is a classic defense in cases where the state is unable to provide a body in an alleged murder. In criminal law the principle is called corpus delicti. Woodyard asserted that the use of Kevin's alleged confession in the case was not sufficient to establish that a person is dead, but that the state had a separate burden to provide substantial independent evidence apart from the confession to either prove the trustworthiness of the confession or to otherwise prove that the defendant had killed an individual.

In support of that argument the defense used the state's own investigation against itself, pointing out that elements of Kevin's confession about Ashley's death had been investigated and proven untrue, this included his statement that she had stabbed herself on the pier at the lake and then gone into the water - the O.S.B.I. never found any evidence to corroborate that version of the story, though they searched the small lake and tested the pier for traces of blood.

On the issue of identifying the remains in the fire, Woodyard acknowledged to the court that in the preliminary hearing phase that the standard of proof is probable cause. He then addressed the court directly to say that it "sits at this level as the trier of fact and it's the court's obligation to determine the credibility of witnesses as well as the reliability and unreliability of evidence."

With regard to Ashley's death, Woodyard said, "Now, we understand that, you know, she has been missing and not heard from since July the 17th. And we have also heard, you know, a variety of other circumstances in this case. We understand, for example, that there were some bone fragments that were found at the property of Curtis Sweat. That at this residence Kevin Sweat, his son, had actually acknowledged, you know, being involved in the fire, but I would note to the court that the evidence of those bone fragments are not identified to any specific individual. They were not tested. They were not tested for D.N.A. They were identified in a general sense by I guess a forensic anthropologist's report that it might be consistent with a female, a young female of a certain age. That, in our view, is not sufficient evidence to establish identity that's required for probable cause at preliminary."

He continued, "There's one other issue that really hasn't been touched on, although it's now before the court and in the form of the D.N.A. report regarding the burnt tissue that was presented. And I think that's Exhibit 2, if I'm not mistaken submitted by the state. And I would just say this, Your Honor, the report does not reflect that the D.N.A. establishes that this is Ashley Taylor, it's a partial profile. What that means is that typically the scientists have like a thirteen location called Loci, L-O-C-I, where they do testing to get particular genetic markers and they put these markers, called alleles, into those locations. They get a known profile and then they have this unknown profile where they try to make sure that the numbers match in both locations. It's a very simplistic statement of what they do. It's a very complicated science and I certainly am not an expert."

"By a partial profile that means that of these typical thirteen locations, they haven't got readings on all of those, and as a result of that, Your Honor, what they're doing is saying we have this large number on a statistical probability, that they want the court to consider regarding the issue of identity. The problem with that is they cannot identify what the next number will be. And if any of these other numbers, for example, we don't have it as part of the report, but let's assume seven of the thirteen places that she have readings. What about the eighth place? If that, if that is not the same as the known profile, it's one hundred percent excluded. And they can't say that.

"So our primary objection for preliminary hearing purposes on using statistical probability in a D.N.A. report is that it relies on unreliable information because it assumes facts not in evidence and that cannot be proven.

"The second area I think is even more problematic, and that has to do with the issue of homicide. The court is aware homicide is one person killing another person. Typically, it's established through the testimony of a pathologist, the medical examiner.

"As the court reads Exhibit 1, the court will note that the medical examiner said the cause of death and the manner of death is uncertain in this case. So that report provides really no evidentiary value to the court in regarding to two issues, that the death was unlawful, and was caused by the defendant.

"The court has what the State has alleged is a confession. The court heard the circumstances in a general sense of what the confession consists of. And we're really talking about what is referred as corpus delicti. In fairly recent changes with the court of criminal appeals in the Fontenot case, the court did establish that the use of a confession could be sufficient to establish that the defendant, not that a person is dead, that has to be set separate, independent evidence, but that the defendant is a person who might have killed that individual.

"But to do that, under the United States case, Supreme Court case of Opers vs. U.S., the court must find that a confession be supported by a substantial independent evidence that would tend to establish its trustworthiness.

"The court has heard in this case that there's no evidence that the state can point to that establishes the trustworthiness of his statement. There are no cameras that show that he and Ashley Taylor were at that park. There's no evidence of blood on the pier, and there's no body in the lake. This statement is untrustworthy and cannot be used to establish the corpus delicti or the cause or manner of death, and if they can't do that, they can't establish a homicide, at least a homicide or a death by a criminal agency, specifically by Mr. Sweat.

"Those are the issue that we see are of real concern in this case, Your Honor. We don't think that the evidence presented is sufficient enough to support a bind over. For those reasons, we'd ask the court to dismiss the Information."

In fact, the DNA isolated from the burn pile remains was compared to known DNA from Ashley Taylor. The lab reported that the profiles matched and that the probability of selecting an unrelated individual at random from the population having the identical profile was at least one in 2.17 sextillion, according to the medical examiner's report.

Judge Martin did not take long to respond to Woodyard's motion to dismiss. After a brief pause he pronounced, "All right. What I'm going to find then is the State's met its burden of proof regarding the purpose of preliminary hearing. The motion for dismissal, demur will be overruled.

The court has been presented with the evidence that if this young lady had a close relationship with her family. Her mother testified that she was actively involved with their family and allegedly or left to go and get married, or that was their understanding. That as soon as she did not return home on the 29th day, they filed a missing police report.

And the manner of death while I haven't heard that, we do know that based on the probability of the reports entered into, and the recovery, there is sufficient cause to find that the defendant was the one that caused the fire, based upon his father's testimony, that he took the K.S. cup, stuck it in to the side of the house with a drill bit and that he later confronted his son about doing that.

But based upon the totality of the circumstances, all the evidence presented, the state's met its burden of proof. Be bound over to face trial on the amended information on murder in the first degree. District court arraignment will be in front of the Honorable Lawrence Parish as set by him."

The judge concluded by adding one last commentary on the things he had seen and heard over the course of the proceedings, "And I will say this is one of the saddest cases I've had in a long time and tragedy has visited our county. All right. Let me wish you a very good evening and we will stand in recess."


Mike Taylor attended every single court date to see that justice was served for his daughter. He was privy to most of the evidentiary hearings. The lengthy process began to wear on him and the other family members. He remarked, "It's starting to anger me a little bit to see some of those things again. I try to keep those emotions in check which is very hard to do sometimes. I guess we're going to have to see how it plays out."

The grieving father had a difficult time reconciling the man on trial with the same person who dated his daughter. "The Kevin I see in there isn't the Kevin I saw when he was dating my daughter. It isn't the same person. When he sat in my home, at my table, talking to me, that isn't the same Kevin."

But Kevin's chameleon-like characteristics were not just reserved for his appearance. Manipulative behavior is not unusual for domestic abusers. Prosecutors came across evidence that Kevin abused and threatened to kill another woman before the Weleetka murders ever occured. As trial loomed, the investigative team continued to interview Kevin's associates and co-workers in search of information that could show what had motivated him to drive down a dirt road and gun down two little girls. They couldn't accept the assertion that the killing had been purely random. They drove to Tulsa to sit down with one of Kevin's old girlfriends.

When they knocked on the door the girl answered and invited them in. She didn't hesitate to tell the two investigators what she knew about her former paramour. But Maxey and Kurt couldn't help but notice as she recounted the details, the woman had a mannequin on display in her living room, dressed in lingerie. It was the elephant in the room, so to speak, but the pair stayed focused on the task at hand. After they concluded the interview the two walked back out to Kurt's O.S.B.I. vehicle and got in to make the trek back home. They looked at each other, incredulous. "What was that about?" Maxey inquired. After the long hours of detective work and dozens of solved cases, this was one question to which Kurt had no answer. The pair had come to expect the bizarre over the course of this investigation. Some elements proved beyond explanation.

The former girlfriend was willing to testify that Kevin began physically and mentally abusing her. According to her account, the couple had been backroading when a disagreement erupted. She reported to Maxey and Kurt that Kevin had pulled out a black semi-automatic handgun and pointed it at her. He threatened to kill her, her family and himself if she tried to end their romance. She told the investigators that she had moved away in order to escape Kevin Sweat.

Despite the apparent strength of the prosecution's case, one issue continued to plague both the investigators and the prosecution. The team was perplexed on the issue of motive. One of the most important pieces of the puzzle was the question of intent in the murders of the little girls. Maxey and Kurt continued to dig for any hint of a clue as the trial loomed ahead. The prosecution could not rest in full confidence of their case without understanding a motive.

## CHAPTER 13

## Judgment Day

*But the fighting time's all over and it's all gone*
*You pick up the pieces and we try to carry on.*
~Pay No Rent, Evan Felker and John Fullbright

**A**fter Judge Martin ruled that the State had met its burden to proceed to trial, the case moved forward to be decided by another judge, Judge Parish. The first step in the process leading up to trial is arraignment in district court, where the defendant appears and is advised about his rights. The time that elapses before the upcoming trial is comprised of conference hearings, motion hearings and negotiations between defense attorneys and the prosecutorial team.

Maxey and Kurt continued to chase down potential motives during the intervening period leading up to trial. Time was running out and the prospect of presenting an incomplete case before the court drove them with an even greater sense of urgency than before. They met witnesses with whom they had already spoken once, and in several cases twice.

Amanda Hamm was one of Kevin's coworkers at Subway with whom the investigators had already met. They combed through notes from the previous conversations and double checked them with Amanda. Near the end of the conversation, having confirmed various facts that were insignificant to the case, Maxey and Kurt began to gather their things. They were near the end of their witness list. It looked as if this one, too, would amount to a dead end.

The two made their way toward the door, when Ms. Hamm mentioned that she remembered one more thing the prosecutor might be interested to hear. Maxey and Kurt sat back down. Amanda told them, as an aside, that Kevin mentioned he hated the Placker family when she worked with him after the Weleetka murders. When Amanda asked why, Kevin told her he believed someone had murdered his brother Brian, the young man who died of a drug overdose. He told Hamm that Brian had obtained the drugs from the Placker family. He believed they were responsible somehow. Another woman who worked at Subway during the same time corroborated Amanda's account.

Maxey was stunned. She could not understand how Kevin's coworker had failed to mention this detail in previous interviews or how she had failed to grasp its import. It was the missing piece for which they had been grappling over the course of four long years.

She and Kurt immediately set up a meeting with Christopher Placker, who was serving a prison sentence for drug charges. When they sat down with him in prison, the young man was earnest in his desire to assist with the investigation. He had been devastated by his sister's murder, just like the rest of the Placker family.

Maxey sat down across from Christopher and began to convey the story she had just been told by Amanda Hamm. She showed the young man pictures of Brian Sweat and asked if perhaps Christopher had any recollection of meeting Kevin's brother. The young man appeared shocked at the initial question, then his face washed white. He put his head in his hands and began to sob. When he regained composure, he confirmed to Maxey and Kurt that he did recognize Brian Sweat's photograph. He recalled having been in the same circles during that time. The lifestyle the two men lived meant they ran with the same people. Their paths had intersected several times. Whether or not he specifically sold to Brian, Christopher could not recall. No one had any way of verifying whether those were the same drugs that caused Brian Sweat's overdose, or even that Christopher had ever sold anything to Brian. But Christopher was wrecked by the possible connection, nonetheless.

The investigators gathered their things to go, satisfied that they had discovered Kevin Sweat's elusive motive at last. As they walked away, Taylor Placker's big brother called them back for one last word. When Maxey turned to face him once more, he looked her in the eye and said, "If he ever comes in here, I'll kill him."

Armed at last with the criminal element they so desperately needed to present a solid case, the prosecution filed court documents to reflect that Amanda Hamm and Christopher Placker agreed to testify. Those documents reflected the general nature of their testimony, that these two witnesses would testify under oath Kevin blamed the Placker family for the death of his own brother.

Throughout the pre-trial proceedings, the prosecution had pressured the defense by pointing out the strength of their overwhelming evidence. One of the best retorts in the defense's arsenal had been a lack of motive. More than once in negotiations, Kevin's team argued, "Our client simply had no reason to kill two small children." Now, with the wind taken out of their sails, the defense team responded almost immediately to the new revelation. On July 31, 2014, they entered a blind plea of guilty to each of the three murders. In exchange for the guilty plea, Kevin made one request: he wanted to meet with the F.B.I. During the initial hearing in which Sweat submitted the guilty plea in person, the judge asked if he was pleading guilty without coercion and of his own free will. Kevin answered yes. The judge then asked if he was satisfied with his representation and Sweat again confirmed that he was. The judge set the sentencing hearing for October 24, 2014.

The exact details of just what Kevin discussed with the F.B.I. remain unknown. What is known, is that federal agents met with Sweat according to his request at least once. That following Friday, however, Kevin decided to try and withdraw his guilty plea stating in a cryptic, handwritten note that the "F.B.I. agents didn't find anything." The judge refused his request to withdraw the plea.

With sentencing at hand in mere months, Kevin reached out to the press in desperation. He focused on one reporter in particular, Phil Cross from Fox 25. He began by telling Cross that his lawyers told him he could not discuss the mess he was in. It was a strangely personal letter, one in which he greeted the reporter in a manner expected of a close acquaintance.

The news channel took the writings to a criminologist at the University of Central Oklahoma. She determined that the letter appeared to be the words of a narcissist, desperate to get himself out of trouble. The criminologist surmised that Kevin viewed the reporter as "the Lone Ranger" who could help him escape his circumstances.

Kevin continued to contact Phil Cross, by telephone and letter in the months leading up to sentencing. He told Cross that he had evidence of other crimes. Kevin discussed D.N.A. evidence and also the handwriting on the cross at the memorial site as evidence of his innocence. But when pressed about the damning evidence against him, including the axe in his vehicle with Ashley's D.N.A. on it and the ownership of the glock, Kevin was loathe to speak. Despite their correspondence Cross maintained objectivity. He, like many others associated with the case, despaired that Kevin's past remained in large part a mystery to those attempting to find any sort of explanation for the events that took place.

Kevin ultimately claimed that in the O.S.B.I. recordings, Agent Titsworth had dressed someone up to look like him during the interviews wherein he confessed to killing Placker, Whitaker, and Taylor. He stated that he provided this information to the FBI when he met with them but they failed to believe or act on his story.

For at least one criminal profiler, even after the guilty plea, some doors from the investigation had been left open. Dr. Brent Turvey said, "in a real case run by serious professionals you put the gun in the defendant's hand and you put the projectiles fired from that gun into the victim." The profiler had offered his opinion of the case early on, before Sweat was ever a suspect. The profile did not rule out Sweat but it certainly had not married well with the state's case. The profile stated that the perpetrator would be motivated by anger and sexual motivation. He wrote that the anger was directed at Taylor. It also indicated that the killer had a low level of criminal skill and likely had some sort of relationship with the victims. Turvey observed that the killer would be experienced with firearms. The elements of the profile that were most at odds with the state's findings surmised that the girls had not been murdered in the ditch where they were found.

In addition Turvey wrote that at least two people approached the girls and that one of them struck Taylor in the face, likely with the butt of the gun. He said the trajectory of the bullets would have been impossible had the bodies not been moved. The piece of evidence most indicative of that conclusion was the gunshot wound found under Taylor's shorts, though the shorts themselves had not been damaged. From this, Dr. Turvey concluded that Taylor's shorts must have been put back on her after the murders occurred.

Turvey felt obligated to weigh in yet again after Kevin pled guilty. "The person who would have killed these girls; the motivation was a lot more anger and it was directed only at one of the girls and not necessarily both of them." "He's got mental issues. He's not a healthy person mentally and I don't think anybody fully understands what those mental health issues are."

On the day of sentencing Kevin waited in his holding cell. He had expressed his desire to attend a meeting among the attorneys that morning but he was asked to wait instead. His attorney requested that his client's handcuffs be removed before they entered the court, for the sake of his own dignity and in recognition of his guilty plea. As he had before, the judge agreed and Kevin Sweat's hands were once again set free.

The Okfuskee Courthouse is a very old yet dignified little building, typical of small town Oklahoma. The corridors are rather grey and dim, and the spaces are very narrow so that everyone, prosecuted and prosecutors alike, move in the same spaces sandwiched in and a bit too close for comfort. Most Oklahoma courthouses are not at all similar to the typical scenes in a movie. Often times defense attorneys meet with their clients at old public school desks set up in the hall, caught up in client-attorney discussion that all can overhear. In reality, witnesses, defendants, prosecutors and the public come face to face in the cramped halls of justice.

Maxey was preparing to enter the judge's chambers that day when she walked up on Kevin and two of the members from his defense team, Wayne and Peter. They had gathered in a very small room at the end of a narrow hall. Gretchen was in the nearby court reporter's office along with

Maxey, the other Assistant District Attorney and the DA Investigator Craig Hicks. As the defense team walked together a flurry of activity erupted amongst the group of men. Kevin Sweat, in one rapid movement, threw his freed hands up and around Peter Astor's throat. Astor instinctively threw his own hands up to block the attack, but Sweat was successful at dragging a razor across his attorney's neck.

At the first sign of violence Maxey shouted, "Oh, hell!" She took off in a sprint away from the struggling men. Investigator Hicks launched himself from the court reporter's office onto Kevin, breaking his nose and his glasses. Hicks brought Kevin back under control and the courtroom was placed on lockdown. Maxey returned as soon as it became evident that the violence was over. The guards conducted a thorough search of Kevin's person, then he was dressed again and court resumed.

Shaking and bleeding, but with no life threatening injuries, Kevin handed a note to the judge which read,

*"I'm withdrawing my guilty plea because the primary reason I entered my plea was to speak to the FBI about possible crimes committed by the O.S.B.I. and because of the FBI's lack of finding I'm wanting to withdraw. The FBI was the only reason I entered the blind plea cause they didn't want to get involved with my case but now cause they weren't able to discover anything. Plus people indicating*

*their statements were being twisted. If the State is
confident in their cases, then they got nothing to
worry about." [Signed] Kevin Sweat, 10-24-14"*

    Courthouse security had searched Kevin
before the incident. Officials surmised that he
smuggled the razor in his mouth. Astor was cut and
bleeding from his neck but he did not require
hospitalization. In a near-superhuman act of
professionalism, he asked to be excused from court
to avoid the possibility of influencing the judge
during sentencing with his bloodied appearance.
His efforts, while gallant, made no difference in the
court's decision. Kevin Sweat was sentenced to
three life sentences without the possibility of parole.
The sentences were to run consecutively, one after
another. In Oklahoma, Sweat is required to serve
85% of each sentence prior to becoming eligible for
parole consideration. When the judge announced
that the sentences would run consecutively he
announced, "This was judgment day."

    After he attacked Peter Astor, Kevin sent
another letter to reporter Phil Cross and wrote, "I
had no intentions on killing Peter," and that his
intention behind the attack was to get his attorney
to "confess" to what he considered lies and
misrepresentations. Sweat went on to tell Cross
that he had intended to have Cross brought in with
Fox 23's cameras to record Astor's "confession".
He wrote of the delusional plan, "I had a feeling it
probably wouldn't have worked at all but if anything

it showed I wasn't scared of a grown man." The entire debacle was a pathetic derivative of that old film he and Ashley had been obsessed with when they had first fallen in love: *Natural Born Killers*.

After the attack on the defense team, Maxey went on to do her job. But that afternoon Claudia received a call. She had been on vacation in New Mexico with her new love, Andy, when the phone rang. She knew it was Maxey on the other line, but what she was saying was unintelligible. Claudia feared the worst, that perhaps something awful had happened to a family member. She explained to her young friend, "Honey, you have to calm down, I can't understand what you're saying to me." On the other line, Maxey continued to sob. She didn't just release the emotion of a violent attack in her workplace, which she had long feared, she also allowed the pent up grief of the entire case erupt to her trusted friend. When she was finished crying she went out to the lake and poured herself a glass of wine.

When the families of Taylor Placker, Skyla Whitaker and Ashley Taylor received the news that Kevin had been sentenced to life without parole, a great release of emotion erupted outside the courthouse. Several of them searched out Maxey Reilly to embrace her and personally express their sheer gratitude for a final sense of justice; for a brief moment of freedom from grief. But the victim's families also made it clear that there would be no "normal" for them ever again, even after the courtroom triumph.

Ashley Taylor's family was understandably upset because not only had she been murdered, but she had been accused of some actions for which she could not defend herself. The allegations Kevin made during his confessions disturbed the family in particular. They objected to his accusation that Ashley practiced Wicca, that the couple practiced Wicca together, and that somehow that may have caused him to hallucinate and see the two little girls as monsters, as he described them in the confession tape. As far as the Taylor family knew, she had never been involved in anything of the sort. Rather, they remembered a loving daughter who looked after her disabled siblings with tenderness. They remembered her own innocence as a child and mourned her lost chance to become a mother. Mike Taylor expressed an inkling of the family's anger and sorrow in a letter for the Victim's Impact Statement. It is re-published here exactly as he wrote it:

*As with all parents, even after their children are grown. Ashley always has been and always will be "My" Little Girl.*

*To completely articulate how Ashley's Death has affected my life would be impossible.*

*Just sitting down to write this is extremely painful.*

*Some of my fondest memories of Ashley occurred while she was a child. Watching her race around hunting easter eggs. The smile and excitement on her face on Christmas morning. Sitting down and watching cartoons with her as she told me about each and every character.*

*Reading her stories at bedtime and having her correct me if I changed it in any way.*

*The look she gave me one morning when I was heading out to go deer hunting, having her point her finger at me and telling me I was not allowed to hunt Bambi or Bambis' mother. The look on her face the time a giraffe stuck his head in the car and she fed it by hand.*

*How she would crawl into my lap and hug me tightly around the neck when she was tired and ready for a nap. And my favorite memory of all, the first time I laid my eyes on her, the day she was born.*

*Since Ashley's death, I find more often than not. The memories that I love and cherish are now being overshadowed with memories of Death, Grief, Lies, and Deceit.*

*Memories of the Trauma going through the Criminal Justice System. Memories of the awful things that were said about my Wife and I, By people who do not know us, as well as by some we considered friends. Memories of the day I was told she was missing along with all that transpired that day. Memories of how the investigation progressed including how we officially found out how Ashley was murdered (via the Internet). Memories of the condition of her remains when found. Memories I did not ask for! Memories I do not deserve!*

*The memories surrounding Ashley's Murder are now something I re-live over and over while trying to sleep. The recurring nightmares now fuel the insomnia I deal with on a regular basis. For the first time in my life, I now find myself having to seek medical attention and take medication for depression. No matter how hard you try to hide the pain it will always find a way to surface. For me I began to notice this while filling out a report, following a response to a very traumatic incident. A doctor and nurse both called attention to and asked why my hand was shaking. At times it has gotten to the point that I can't even hold my cell phone without dropping it.*

*As a paramedic of 20-plus years, I now wonder how much longer I will be able to continue working in the field now. That traumatic events seem to have a negative impact on me both physically and psychologically.*

*I find myself becoming more and more distant with friends, relatives and co-workers.*

*Special occasions such as Holidays, Birthdays, Christmas and Thanksgiving no longer have the same meaning to me. The only thing I think about is not having Ashley around anymore. I miss her smiles, her Laughter and her jokes. I will never hear her voice again or be able to tell her I love her or give her a hug. I will never know the joy of holding my own Grandchild or watch Ashley grow up and reach her full potential. I Love You Ashley and miss you terribly. You always have been and always will be my little girl.*

*Closure:*
*A word I have heard so many times since Ashley's Murder. A word that holds no meaning to me. A word that on its surface sounds like the right thing to say. A word that holds more meaning to the person saying it. The pain of Ashley's Murder is Real, the psychological affects are real. The illness and maladies I now suffer are Real. The nightmares and memories are real. I do not believe that there can ever be any real "Closure". The best I can ever hope for is for Justice to be served appropriately and for me to find a way to cope "with what no Father should ever endure" for the rest of my life!!"*

Kevin acquired a new attorney after his sentencing and set out to appeal his sentence. During the proceedings he was allowed to take the stand for the first time to ask to withdraw his guilty plea. Astor, Woodyard and Mosley had withdrawn from further representation of Sweat, on the likelihood that they would be called as witnesses in the razor incident.

The appeal went to the Oklahoma Court of Criminal Appeals using an argument of ineffective assistance of counsel. He argued that his defense team had lied to him about the circumstances surrounding his .22 rifle. Sweat stated that the State claimed that he had used his .22 rifle to shoot Taylor and Skyla. He further pointed out that he had spoken with the individual that sold him the rifle and the individual remembered the transaction, but, he argued, defense counsel told him that the individual told them he had no recollection at all of selling the firearm.

Kevin complained that he felt his defense counsel had given up on him one year before his plea deal, because they had begun to "just focus on, for lack of better terms, an insanity defense." He made a regular habit of complicating an already impossible situation for his defense team. He spoke to reporters and officials with abandon in spite of counsel to the contrary. He told a Corrections Department probation officer that he had not shot the girls, even after his guilty plea. He told the same officer that Ashley was killed in a struggle over a gun when she became upset that he wouldn't marry her. The probation officer documented their conversation in a report in which he stated that the defendant was "unsure who pulled the trigger," but that he saw "little or no remorse by the defendant about the death of his girlfriend." When the officer inquired how Ashley's remains came to be in a burnpile Kevin surmised he may have "blacked out."

Sweat asserted that Dr. Brent Turvey's early criminal profile did not match his own and that the absence of a bullet hole in Taylor's shorts proved the girls' bodies had been moved. He also pointed out that DNA fragments found in one of the girls' underwear did not match his own and thus proved a motive for someone else. Kevin also argued that the handwriting analysis on the memorial cross did not match his own. In later writings, Kevin would opine that two of his girlfriends had recanted their testimony about his statements regarding the murders.

But the appellate court would have none of it, writing that, "Petitioner (Sweat) shot and killed two young girls and left their bodies in a bar ditch. He killed his fiance of four years so that she would not reveal his involvement in the girls' deaths. He disposed of his fiance's remains, leaving behind only small fragments of her person. ... It is only through the zealous representation of defense counsel, that Petitioner avoided the possibility of multiple death sentences."

# CHAPTER 14

# The Judge

*Hoping everyone there will be left alone*
*Safe and sound when I get home*
*Telling stories about the good ole days*
*Where everyone I know and love is safe*
~Wild Bird, Carter Sampson

Kevin Sweat was sent to serve out his
sentences in "Big Mac", the highest security prison
in Oklahoma. The prison was built in 1908 to house
maximum security inmates and death row
prisoners. He arrived there on November 12, 2014
with two convictions of first degree murder and one
conviction of second degree murder. The State
later pursued him for his 2017 courtroom assault on
Peter Astor. He was convicted of Assault and
Battery with a Deadly Weapon and received an

additional sentence of sixty years on top of the three life sentences. He continues to decry the justice system through written correspondence. After participating with a production company's documentary about the case, Kevin claims he is no longer able to participate in interviews at the prison. He also states in writing that the last of his friends have ceased communication and that the only person left to make regular contact is his mother.

Kurt Titsworth received accolades for his work as lead agent in the Weleetka murders. The O.S.B.I. named him the 2011 Agent of the Year. In a press release announcing the award the agency wrote, "For more than three years, Kurt has worked the killings of two young girls in Okfuskee County while working a full caseload. The day Taylor Placker and Skyla Whitaker were gunned down he began running leads. Although agents flooded the area for months, it became evident that justice would take delicate time to attain. With measured humility and grace, he continued to keep the victims' families informed of progress." Kurt continues to serve the people of Oklahoma in the O.S.B.I.

After six years passed the time had come for Taylor and Skyla's classmates at the now-consolidated Graham-Dustin public schools to graduate. They left an empty chair to remind all those in attendance that the girls' absence was not been forgotten. Nine seniors graduated that night. Taylor would have been the only remaining student present from the original class at Graham public school.

The school principal continues to deal with the trauma of losing two beloved students, though the new children coming in to the school are peacefully oblivious to the tragedy that once befell the community. The students take field trips to the Henryetta library, where they read the book, 'Jumpy the Turtle', which was written in honor of the girls whose lives were so devoted to their animals, and always insisted on saving turtles. The principal said as she heard the story read out loud, she was brought to tears once again. She was struck as she looked around, by the realization that these children were too young to know about the circumstances of loss that inspired the book.

Outside the schoolhouse stands a garden memorial festooned with hostas, purple petunias, butterflies and frog figurines. An Ohio man who never met Taylor and Skyla, donated the materials and traveled to Oklahoma to build it. A woman from Arkansas donated a birdbath. The memorial is situated next to the school's playground equipment, from whence joy and laughter once again fills the air.

Skyla's parents continued to work at the school. After Kevin pled guilty they declined any presence in the press, choosing instead to grieve in private. The Plackers, too, had long since grown weary of the repeated questioning and rehashing of June 8th's horrific details. They issued a statement after the sentencing came down, saying, "Now we know for sure (Sweat's) the one who did it."

Ashley Taylor's mother said, "knowing that she's not there, it's hard every single day. They say it gets easier. It doesn't get any easier. Every night before we go to bed we have pictures on the wall and we blow her kisses and tell her we love her. We just talk about her all the time."

Today, Ashley's best friend Anna remains in large part the skinny, dark-haired exile from their youth. She still sketches, paints and smokes. She walks in the room with the smell of stale smoke and slightly stooped shoulders, as if shouldering a burden. She doesn't wear makeup or a bra, and her hair is pulled back tightly away from her face. Her fingernails are kept short, almost to the quick, but you can see she works with her hands because there is dirt beneath her nails. Despite, or perhaps because of, her unconventional appearance, Anna is a fetching and magnetic woman with a genuine, but somewhat melancholy demeanor. Her dark eyes sparkle on the odd happenstance of a smile. She wears a faded black t-shirt and a pair of jeans. It's a getup she claims to have been wearing for a week straight. She says it identifies her immediately as an Okmulgee girl. Across the front of the shirt is a bear and the word EZEKIEL. In small print below it the shirt reads "ALL WE HAVE IS NOW".

Anna recalls the last couple of times Ashley reached out to contact her. Anna stopped responding to Ashley's messages after being contacted to bring over marijuana but not being welcomed in the house. When she declined to answer, Ashley sent another message to say that she was hurt that Anna didn't want to speak with her anymore. The last time Ashley tried to contact her was to let her know of the engagement to Kevin. When Anna still didn't respond, Ashley once again wrote to tell her old friend that she felt hurt.

The Sunday before she disappeared Ashley was spotted at the church she had once attended with Anna. She was in tears that day, though no one knows why. When the preacher gave the altar call Ashley went to the altar and fell on her knees, weeping. No one knows why she cried or what she prayed for that day. Anna thinks that Ashley was afraid and may have known that something sinister lay in her future. She believes that Ashley's demeanor perhaps indicated that her life had gone out of control. One of the hardest realizations in life is to accept that some questions will never be answered.

Today Anna remains a dedicated artist. She hopes that one day she can reconnect with her best friend. Until that day, she has reached an uneasy inner truce with the tragic events that took not one, but two good friends away from her. To this day she continues to feel torn for everyone involved in the tragic events that played out in her hometown, including Kevin Sweat. She believes he needed interventional help that he just didn't get in time. Anna laments that her friends have been reduced to one-dimensional characters in a sensational story, without the true-life details that complicate judgment. Of her friends, she says, "Life is just a big sliding scale when you get down to it. They didn't play it safe enough to get a chance to grow up."

Maxey carried on in the D.A.'s office for several years after Kevin Sweat's incarceration. Her work continued to demonstrate a tough-as-nails approach and a non-discriminatory drive to prosecute crime. She took on a case that exposed an Oklahoma State Trooper after he was accused of three separate incidents of improper sexual contact with women he had pulled over. No one else wanted to touch the case because the officer had worked with a great number of officials over the years and established connections with powerful people. Maxey did not hesitate.

By 2016, she decided it was time to retire from the District Attorney's office. Her two children reached active ages in the public school and time spent in support of their activities began to take priority. Also, the constant stress and anxiety of the position had taken its toll over the years. She entered private practice in Okemah right down on Main Street.

People outside the community began to take note of her dedication. The years of mostly thankless public service produced a reputation for fearlessness, drive, commitment to justice and an unwavering desire to see it applied blindly. News of her work reached the highest levels of Oklahoma state government over time. When the Associate District Judge of Okfuskee County retired, Maxey carefully considered the position. She very much enjoyed relative anonymity during the short stint in private practice. But she spoke to her husband about the prospect, and with his support, Maxey decided to seek the judgeship. She believed it was the very thing she was meant to do. By that time she had over thirty jury trials under her belt. She felt confident that she would make a good and fair judge. After all those years of being underestimated by others, she knew she could put aside public opinion and make decisions based on evidence and the law. She had spent a lifetime, after all, of being judged harshly.

During the selection process she had to appear before a judicial nominating committee, comprised of a group of attorneys and average citizens from across the state. She sat at one end of the table and faced the group, gathered together at the other end. The committee grilled her with inquiries for about forty minutes with questions that spanned every aspect of her life, from age 19 forward. The committee selected Maxey and two other candidates to go to the Capitol and meet with the Governor. The Governor selected Maxey to take the seat. She was the youngest district judge in the entire state of Oklahoma.

In naming Maxey to the judgeship the governor noted that she had been very active in starting up Okfuskee County's drug court, a program that sought to rehab drug offenders rather than incarcerate them. Based on her work in the Weleetka murders she was named the O.S.B.I.'s law enforcement agent of the year. Bikers Against Child Abuse named her prosecutor of the year in 2014. Noting Maxey's involvement in the community outside the law, including President of the Chamber of Commerce and the PTA, the governor wrote, "Maxey Reilly will serve the residents of Okfuskee County well. She has an exceptional knowledge of the law, and has the acumen and temperament necessary to be a successful judge."

In response Maxey wrote, "I want to use my knowledge and experience to positively impact as many people as possible...I am extremely honored to serve the people of Okfuskee County as associate district judge."

The day of her swearing in, Maxey's family filed in dressed in their finest clothes. There, gathered in a a fine courtroom paneled in dark walnut, Maxey's mother, sisters, father and step mother looked on. Her husband, the man who remained at her side through the darkest of nights, ushered in their two gorgeous children who beamed with pride at their mother. There too, were many members of the local community, eager to show their gratitude for the service the young attorney had given their town. Maxey took her oath and looked out at the audience of around a hundred people. She choked back a moment of emotion at the beginning of her remarks and then, in characteristic fashion, plowed ahead in that thick Okie drawl, with a speech that promised the people of Okfuskee County that she would use the prominence of her seat in fairness and in promotion of justice for all. She was surrounded by powerful men of the judgeship, state and federal legislative seats, all there to conduct the solemn ceremony for the position which had been chosen by the Governor of the State of Oklahoma. She stood among them, a diminutive thing in that long black judge's robe, and there she held court. Surely there existed not a doubt in the room that she would do exactly as she promised.

Even after all she accomplished, all the trials, the judgeship, some still felt compelled to underestimate. Someone online commented on her photo under the governor's press release writing, "she's too pretty to be taken seriously." An old law school classmate chimed in with a message to a mutual friend asking with incredulity, "did i just read that *MAXEY REILLY* has just been named a judge??" On internet message boards after the announcement people took to the comments section to post crude comments about her physical appearance, her reputation, etc. She decided to eschew social media, for as much as she knows the people who wrote those things are likely not contributing much worth into the social fabric, she remains that little girl from Atoka, Oklahoma at heart. Cruel words can still sting even the most seasoned of judges.

After the swearing-in ceremony Claudia hosted a proper soiree for the new judge at her place out near the lake. She found new love and married again after Ronnie's loss. She and her husband now shared a beautiful home overlooking the water. Every table top and countertop was covered with some sort of cake, cheese trays, lovely looking desserts, balloons and banners all congratulating the prosecutor who had now become the judge. Claudia set up an adult drinks station out back, stocked with champagne of course, but also some homemade wine. It was perhaps a few steps above doe party status, but Maxey's friends weren't about to let her slip into a judge's robe and out of her old country ways. Not that she ever wanted to, anyway.

Maxey obliged the revelers, and moved amongst the various cliques of family, attorneys, local businesspeople and admirers. She was delighted by the celebration and chatted with a shining smile on her face, taking in the moment of accomplishment. On occasion though, she stared off to some distant place, even with the social whir going on all around. It was almost as if she might rather be out fishing on Buckeye Creek.


Ten years after the Weleetka murders and nearly five years after she put the killer in prison, Maxey's days are not quite as anxious as they once were. She and Rob still live at their fanciful place on the lake. The schedule of a district judge is somewhat more flexible than that of a prosecutor. She is always involved in her children's activities, both of them beautiful and talented in their own right. She never misses a piano recital or a basketball game. She still can't allow herself to let the children ride off on their own. Even ten years can't erase some things.

She continues to love the little town of Woody Guthrie, although she can hardly go out to lunch without being interrupted by members of the community. These days there doesn't seem to be so much hostility as there once was. Sure, she still has to put up with the same tired, small town gossip that goes on in every other community across the United States. But now, more often than not, the people who approach her in public want to shake her hand and visit with the distinguished judge, who proved after all to be more of a protector to the community than a punisher.

She is always quick with a smile and a greeting for anyone who stops by. But make no mistake, retreating back to her secluded lake place remains the goal at the end of each day.

She most recently made a quick stop through Subway, she had to grab lunch on the go that day, when a familiar family came walking in together. It was the Placker family. Peter and Vicky had just picked up their son from serving out his prison sentence in McAlester. One could call the encounter serendipitous, but it is a small town. Still, Maxey felt strange to see them with their son. It was a bittersweet reunion, knowing they had one child back but could never truly be whole again without little Taylor. They exchanged respect and formalities. A great, encompassing moment passed between she and the family that was heavy with a shared decade of loss, grief, guilt, desperation and justice.

Most of the bad dreams have left her now. But sometimes after she puts the children to bed she steps out onto the veranda and listens to the night sounds. The owls are always calling to each other on a dark night in Okfuskee County, along with the coyotes. The frogs and cicadas sing with abandon. On occasion a yowling bobcat can be heard. None of the familiar sounds frighten her - she's always prepared to defend her family. But once in a while she sits down alone with a glass of wine and allows her mind to wander. That's when some of the memories come back.

Throughout the investigative process Kurt interviewed Kevin multiple times. Maxey reviewed the confession video over and over in preparation for trial, always focused on the part where Kevin said under questioning that he had shot "the monsters" that day in June. But he also mentioned another detail. During one of his denials Kevin admitted he had been at the crime scene, but not until after the murders. He claimed he had been at his grandfather's house and heard police cars go past. Kevin said he went up the road to find a crowd of people grouped behind the yellow crime scene tape. He walked up, he said, and stood shoulder to shoulder with the spectators hoping to get a glimpse of what was going on.

Long after the trial was over Maxey recalled pulling up to the scene that night, along with her boss. When she got out of the vehicle she had to wait while the officer checked a list of names to verify that she was allowed inside the tape. She stood next to a group of onlookers gathered there. If Kevin's account of that day held any kernel of truth then it is quite possible he went back to the crime scene and watched, blended in with the crowd that evening. The possibility remains that Maxey stood shoulder to shoulder with the killer that night. Together they would have viewed the scene of the little girls as they lay there, all four with an interconnectedness rooted more deeply than any of them could have ever wanted.

She remembered.

**Judge Maxey Parker Reilly**

# SOURCES BY CHAPTER

*A Note From the Author*
Much of the information used in the creation of this novel came from multiple interviews conducted over the course of two years with Judge Maxey Parker Reilly, with whom I attended the University of Oklahoma College of Law, and Agent Kurt Titsworth of the O.S.B.I.

It should also be noted that I exchanged several letters in communication with D.O.C. Inmate Kevin Sweat.

A great deal of facts were gathered from an army of dedicated reporters, who did the hard, in-person work of documenting the days that came after the homicides and the long years that followed. I am indebted and grateful to these writers and colleagues.

The entirety of the preliminary hearing's quoted dialogue and a great deal of narrative came from the Transcript of Proceedings in Okfuskee County, had on the 28th and 29th days of January 2013.

## Chapter 2: Okfuskee County
"The 2016 U.S. census" from The United States Census Bureau,
https://factfinder.census.gov/faces/tableservices/jsf/pages/productview.xhtml?src=CF

"The iron horse charged through" paraphrased from
Oklahoma Historical Society, Weleetka entry.
www.okhistory.org/publications/enc/entry.php?entry
=WE010

"Friends and brothers" from Kane, Sharyn and
Keeton, Richard (1994). "As Long As Grass Grows
[Ch. 11]". Fort Benning: The Land and the People.
Fort Benning, GA and Tallahassee, FL. U.S. Army
Infantry Center, Directorate of Public Works,
Environmental Management Division, and National
Park Service, Southeast Archaeological Center. Pp.
95-104

Collins, Rob. "Picture of Horror" *Oklahoma Gazette*.
24 May 11

**Chapter 3: They Killed Our Babies**
Official Transcript of Proceedings, January 28th
and 29th, 2013, In the District Court of Okfuskee
County, State of Oklahoma. State of Oklahoma v.
Kevin Sweat. CF-11-126 and C-2014-930. Volume
I, Witness Testimony of Peter Placker. pp. 9-60

From Johnson, Johnny. "For Slain Weleetka Girls'
Kin, Pain Keeps Coming" *The Oklahoman*. 12 Jun
08. Web:
https://newsok.com/article/3256335/for-slain-girls-ki
n-pain-keeps-coming

**Chapter 4: "The Long Days After"**
"Agent Brad Greene...", from p. 66.
"five spent Winchester .40 caliber..." from pp. 67.
"the sheets that covered the bodies..." from pp. 68.
"the majority of the discarded shells..." from pp. 72.
"nine hundred and sixty seven feet north..." from p. 75
"two of the wounds to her face were noticeably smaller..." from pp. 77
"did not find any .22 shell casings at the scene..." from pp. 84

Official Transcript of Proceedings, January 28th and 29th, 2013, In the District Court of Okfuskee County, State of Oklahoma. State of Oklahoma v. Kevin Sweat. CF-11-126 and C-2014-930. Volume I, Witness Testimony Agent Brad Green. Pp. 61-97

"Peter was in an emotional state such that he could not bring himself to recount specific details about walking up on the girls that day" from Juozapavicius, Justin. "Two Girls Shot Dead In Small Oklahoma Town" 11 Jun 08. A.P. Web: http://helenair.com/news/national/two-girls-shot-dead-in-small-oklahoma-town/article_a759c5da-39e7-547a-b79b-7e6a1466ff69.html

"One of the many theories" from Sutter, John. "New Sketch Fuels Hope In Slayings" *The Oklahoman*. 14 Jun 08. Web:

https://newsok.com/article/3257467/new-sketch-fue
ls-hope-in-slayings

"what the threat is" from Grinberg, Emmanuella.
"Shooting deaths of Oklahoma girls remain a
mystery one year later" CNN.com. 8 Jun 09. Web:
www.cnn.com/2009/CRIME/06/08/oklahoma.girls.m
ystery/index.html

"pink and white carnations." from Jackson, Ron.
"Slain Girl Mourned in First Funeral of the Day". *The
Oklahoman*. 13 Jun 2008. Web:
http://newsok.com/article/3257029/slain-girl-mourne
d-in-first-funeral-of-the-day

"better, not bitter" and "now she will never graduate
…" from Jackson, Ron. "FUNERALS: Nurture Love,
Mourners Told." *The Oklahoman*. 14 Jun 08. Web:
https://newsok.com/article/3257469/funerals-nurtur
e-love-mourners-told

"The unique thing about this town" from Billington,
Jeff. "ID Effort for Girls' Families Ongoing" *The
Tulsa World*. 15 Jun 08. Web:
https://www.tulsaworld.com/news/government/aid-e
ffort-for-girls-families-ongoing/article_f7543e9a-ad0
3-52c9-84d7-5b28c69a7bfb.html

"Classmates from Graham school took donation
jars to surrounding businesses" from Billington,
Jeff. "Weleetka Schools Mourns Slain Girls." *The

*Tulsa World.* 12 Jun 18. Web:
https://www.tulsaworld.com/news/state/weleetka-school-mourns-slain-girls/article_e5452f2e-bfc5-5633-9e6b-05ab3facda57.html

"between one hundred fifty and two hundred leads" from Gamallo, Manny. "Witness Reports Seeing Girls Before Slaying." Tulsa World. 13 Jun 08. Web: https://www.tulsaworld.com/news/state/witness-reports-seeing-girls-before-slaying/article_00fdb04d-f956-58e5-92ff-87b0941c.html

"wanted for questioning, but not necessarily a suspect."
"white Ford or Chevy pickup"
from Sutter, John David. "Investigators Searching for Person of Interest." *The Oklahoman.* 13 Jun 08.

"Residents took to police scanners"
"domestic disturbance at the school"
from Branson, Halley and Johnson, Johnny. "Weleetka Arrest Creates False Hope." *The Oklahoman.* 18 Jun 08.

"he looked as if he didn't belong in the area" from Sutter, John. "New Sketch Fuels Hope In Slayings" *The Oklahoman.* 14 Jun 08. Web: https://newsok.com/article/3257467/new-sketch-fuels-hope-in-slayings

"the memorial was found desecrated" from
Johnson, Johnny. "Ominous Message Left at
Murdered Weleetka Girls' Memorial" *The
Oklahoman.* 16 Jul 08. Web:
https://newsok.com/article/3271005/ominous-mess
age-left-at-murdered-weleetka-girls-memorial

"questions from outsiders" from Johnson, Johnny.
"Hitting A Roadblock in Two Girls' Slaying" T*he
Oklahoman.* 13 Jun 08. Web:
https://newsok.com/article/3256784/hitting-a-roadbl
ock-in-2-girls-slayings

"cut back the number of officers"
"voluntarily handed their guns over for test-firing"
from Gamallo, Manny. "OSBI Cuts Officers On
Weleetka Killings" *The Tulsa World.* 13 Sep 08.
Web:
https://www.tulsaworld.com/news/state/osbi-cuts-off
icers-on-weleetka-killings/article_2740db03-7434-5
04e-90b7-6b4a2a27d9f8.html

"hopefully the billboard will wear on them" from
Gamallo, Manny. "Billboard Will Seek New Clues In
Weleetka Girls' Slayings'" *The Tulsa World.* 26 Sep
08. Web:
https://www.tulsaworld.com/news/state/billboard-se
eks-information-in-girls-killings/article_832a83c6-f8
c8-5219-93e1-335c804ce023.html

## Chapter 5: No Known Suspects

"Officials cautioned that an effective investigation" from Raymond, Ken. "Double Murder Is High Profile, HIgh Pressure For Police" *The Oklahoman.* 12 Jun 08. Web: https://newsok.com/article/3256340/double-murder-is-high-profile-high-pressure-for-police

"including ballistics and DNA" from Gamallo, Manny. "
Murder Probe Builds" *The Tulsa World.* 11 Jun 08. Web: https://www.tulsaworld.com/news/state/murder-pro be-builds/article_6d0b2297-46de-5a35-8625-a6f30 8b65dfa.html

"Rosser called the conference to attempt to dispel" from Johnson, Johnny. "Investigation: No Suspects, officials say" *The Oklahoman.* 11 Jun 08. Web: https://newsok.com/article/3255855/investigation-n o-suspects-officials-say

"A specially trained Labrador Retriever" from Gamallo, Manny. "ATF Dog Scours Scene of Killings; No New Evidence" *Tulsa World.* 26 Jun 08. Web: https://www.tulsaworld.com/news/state/atf-dog-sco urs-scene-of-killings-no-new-evidence/article_0f1f7 1ae-a817-523e-94db-d39321628c90.html

"a tip reporting a truck full of boys"

"They told us they were down there shooting, just like they would have been on any Sunday," from Painter, Bryan. "Around Weleetka, Shock But No Answers" *The Oklahoman*. 11 Jun 08. Web: https://newsok.com/article/3255838/around-weleetka-shock-but-no-answers

"The first boy testified before the grand jury for two hours" from Clay, Nolan and Johnson, Johnny. "Weleetka Witnesses Face Grand Jury" *The Oklahoman*. 4 Sep 08. Web: https://newsok.com/article/3292812/weleetka-witnesses-face-grand-jury

"the agency believed kids had written the message" from Barnard, Matt. "Taunting Note Scrawled on Cross at Slain Weleetka Girls' Memorial" Tulsa World. 16 Jul 08.

"A map of County Line Road and the bridge had been drawn on a marker board." from Sutter, John David. "Investigators Searching for Person of Interest" *The Oklahoman*. 13 Jun 08. Web: https://newsok.com/article/3256954/investigators-searching-for-person-of-interest

"Approximately 90 vehicles were stopped which led to about two dozen tips." from Gamallo, Manny. "Bullet Casings Considered Linked to Double Slaying" *Tulsa World*. 17 Jun 08. Web: https://www.tulsaworld.com/news/state/bullet-casin

gs-considered-linked-to-double-slaying/article_6e0b
c7a1-0d23-58ed-980e-8ce29a068f6f.html

"has some sort of relation to the Creek tribe" from
Johnson, Johnny. "Help With Case Comes Across
Boundary Lines" *The Oklahoman*. 22 Jun 08.

"My god, my god, my baby!" from Branson, Halley
R. "Investigators Call for Weleetka Murder
Witnesses to Step Forward" *The Oklahoman*. 21
Jul 08. Web:

"Agents with the OSBI alone logged over 10,000
hours by August." from Gamallo, Manny. "OSBI
Racking Up Man Hours in Weleetka" *Tulsa World*.
10 Aug 08. Web:
https://www.tulsaworld.com/news/crimewatch/osbi-r
acking-up-man-hours-in-weleetka/article_2b46b913
-bb13-50e7-86b1-37bd4c1f9529.html

"results raised questions" from Johnson, Johnny.
"Autopsy Results Offer Clues In Two Girls' Slayings
Near Weleetka" *The Oklahoman*. 10 Aug 08. Web:
https://newsok.com/article/3281166/autopsy-results
-offer-clues-in-two-girls-slayings-near-weleetka

"speculation that Taylor's killing appeared to be
personal" from Murphy-Milano, Susan. "Murder:
Connecting the Dots More Than Once in Oklahoma
- Part 4. Forbes. Web:

https://www.forbes.com/sites/crime/2011/10/31/mur der-connecting-the-dots-more-than-once-in-oklaho ma-part-4/#5c8d2c4d1354

"lack of cooperation" from Grinburg, Emmanuella. "Shooting deaths of Oklahoma girls remain a mystery one year later." CNN.com. 8 Jun 09 Web: http://www.cnn.com/2009/CRIME/06/08/oklahoma. girls.mystery/index.html

"a grand jury would interview three suspects" from *Tulsa World.* "Suspects in Girls' Slayings Testify" 04 Sep 08. Web: https://www.tulsaworld.com/news/state/suspects-in-girls-slayings-testify/article_24c2cfdc-707d-5584-94 5b-4a48834a56ad.html

Colberg, Sonya and Johnny Johnson. "A Walk To Bad Creek Bridge" NewsOK.com Web: http://ndepth.newsok.com/weleetka

"the OSBI sent out 60 letters to registered owners of .40 caliber" from Gamallo, Manny. "Authorities Test Fire Guns in Girls' Slayings" *Tulsa World.* 18 Aug 08. Web: https://www.tulsaworld.com/archives/authorities-tes t-fire-guns-in-girls-slayings/article_ce51df70-aea6-5 5c1-935a-5458ad11a667.html

"The average starting salary for a police officer" from United State Department of Labor, Bureau of Labor Statistics Web: https://www.bls.gov/oes/current/oes333051.htm


## Chapter 6: A Series of Cages

"The juvenile who shot Landon was convicted of first-degree manslaughter" from Stogsdill, Sheila. "13-year-old Is Sentenced On Henryetta Manslaughter Charge." *The Oklahoman.* 12 Oct 11. Web: https://newsok.com/article/3612739/13-year-old-is-sentenced-on-henryetta-manslaughter-charge

"now we're waiting to see if charges will be filed" from the online blog of Kevin Sweat, Deviant Art, https://josepimorgan.deviantart.com/

"go fly over to Kevin and tell him to call us" Aspinwall, Cary. "Kevin Sweat's long and twisted path to a guilty plea." *The Tulsa World.* 4 Aug 14. Web: https://www.tulsaworld.com/news/specialreports/sweattrial/kevin-sweat-s-long-and-twisted-path-to-a-guilty/article_88c7967e-52cf-5676-879d-b2d7de52f21e.html


"Mike Taylor, learned she was in a relationship"

"was pensive and in fear, and completely closed off the moment her fiance came over to greet me." from Murphy-Milano, Susan. "Murder: Connecting the Dots More Than Once in Oklahoma - Part 1. *Forbes*. 27 Oct 11. Web: https://www.forbes.com/sites/crime/2011/10/27/murder-connecting-the-dots-more-than-once-in-oklahoma-part-1/#1b6c98cc27e6

"never wrote a word of marriage"
"explaining that she made him feel trapped" from Aspinwall, Cary. "Kevin Sweat won't face death penalty in killings of Weleetka girls, fiancee" *The Tulsa World*. 4 Jul 14. Web: "https://www.tulsaworld.com/news/courts/kevin-sweat-won-t-face-death-penalty-in-killings-of/article_320f9865-98f3-5b7f-83c1-5e6408e5f383.html

"but he never mentioned an engagement" from Official Transcript of Proceedings, January 28th and 29th, 2013, In the District Court of Okfuskee County, State of Oklahoma. State of Oklahoma v. Kevin Sweat. CF-11-126 and C-2014-930. Volume I, Witness Testimony Deborah Sweat. pp. 252

## Chapter 7: Sissy Is Going To Be Home

"Agent Titsworth's first encounter" from Official Transcript of Proceedings, January 28th and 29th, 2013, In the District Court of Okfuskee County, State of Oklahoma. State of Oklahoma v. Kevin

Sweat. CF-11-126 and C-2014-930. Volume II, Witness Testimony of Kenneth Titsworth. pp. 184 - 228.

"When Curtis arrived" from from Official Transcript of Proceedings, January 28th and 29th, 2013, In the District Court of Okfuskee County, State of Oklahoma. State of Oklahoma v. Kevin Sweat. CF-11-126 and C-2014-930. Volume I, Witness Testimony of Curtis Sweat. pp. 244 - 251

"Kevin told his Aunt Delinda" from  Official Transcript of Proceedings, January 28th and 29th, 2013, In the District Court of Okfuskee County, State of Oklahoma. State of Oklahoma v. Kevin Sweat. CF-11-126 and C-2014-930. Volume I, Witness Testimony of Delinda Morrison. pp. 90.

"The last time Patricia Taylor saw her daughter" from Official Transcript of Proceedings, January 28th and 29th, 2013, In the District Court of Okfuskee County, State of Oklahoma. State of Oklahoma v. Kevin Sweat. CF-11-126 and C-2014-930. Volume III, Witness Testimony of Patricia Taylor. Pp. 9-41

"Kevin went to his aunt's home" from Official Transcript of Proceedings, January 28th and 29th, 2013, In the District Court of Okfuskee County, State of Oklahoma. State of Oklahoma v. Kevin

Sweat. CF-11-126 and C-2014-930. Volume I, Witness Testimony of Delinda Morrison. pp. 90.

"Mike Taylor confronted Kevin" from Murphy-Milano, Susan. "Murder: Connecting the Dots More Than Once in Oklahoma - Part 4. Forbes. Web: https://www.forbes.com/sites/crime/2011/10/31/murder-connecting-the-dots-more-than-once-in-oklahoma-part-4/#5c8d2c4d1354

"Curtis Sweat found something very curious" from Official Transcript of Proceedings, January 28th and 29th, 2013, In the District Court of Okfuskee County, State of Oklahoma. State of Oklahoma v. Kevin Sweat. CF-11-126 and C-2014-930. Volume I, Witness Testimony of Curtis Sweat. pp. 244

"Kevin volunteered to take Agent Titsworth on a little drive" from from Official Transcript of Proceedings, January 28th and 29th, 2013, In the District Court of Okfuskee County, State of Oklahoma. State of Oklahoma v. Kevin Sweat. CF-11-126 and C-2014-930. Volume III, Witness Testimony of Kenneth Titsworth. pp. 274

**Chapter 8: Answers in Ashes**
"he had just gone over there to check on things" from Official Transcript of Proceedings, January 28th and 29th, 2013, In the District Court of Okfuskee County, State of Oklahoma. State of

Oklahoma v. Kevin Sweat. CF-11-126 and
C-2014-930. Volume I, Witness Testimony of Curtis
Sweat. pp.244

Murphy-Milano, Susan. "Connecting the Dots More
Than Once in Oklahoma" *Forbes*. 30 Oct 11. Web:
https://www.forbes.com/sites/crime/2011/10/31/mur
der-connecting-the-dots-more-than-once-in-oklaho
ma-part-4/#5c8d2c4d1354

"I suppose I'm going to get blamed for this like I did
the two Weleetka girls." *Fox23 News*. 11 Nov 04
Web:
https://www.fox23.com/news/breaking-news/suspec
ted-secrets-in-weleetka-murders/254313235

" they declined to enter the apartment at that time."
Murphy-Milano, Susan. "Connecting the Dots More
Than Once in Oklahoma" *Forbes*. 30 Oct 11. Web:
https://www.forbes.com/sites/crime/2011/10/31/mur
der-connecting-the-dots-more-than-once-in-oklaho
ma-part-4/#5c8d2c4d1354

"So what did you do with your gun?" *Fox23 News*.
13 Dec 11
Web:
https://www.fox23.com/news/breaking-news/accuse
d-killer-kevin-sweat-in-court/254336567

"younger brother and sister who are mentally challenged" from Fox23 News. "Suspected Secrets In Weleetka Murders. 4 Nov 11 https://www.fox23.com/news/breaking-news/suspected-secrets-in-weleetka-murders/254313235

"entered simply to conduct a welfare check" Official Transcript of Proceedings, January 28th and 29th, 2013, In the District Court of Okfuskee County, State of Oklahoma. State of Oklahoma v. Kevin Sweat. CF-11-126 and C-2014-930. Volume II, Witness Testimony of Lyndon Spears. pp. 131 - 166

"Faye Taylor drove out to the apartment" "98% sure was Ashley Taylor." from Murphy-Milano, Susan. "Connecting the Dots More Than Once in Oklahoma" *Forbes*. 30 Oct 11. Web: https://www.forbes.com/sites/crime/2011/10/31/murder-connecting-the-dots-more-than-once-in-oklahoma-part-4/#5a52047a1354

"What they did find was 20% of a normal human skeleton by weight" from Board of the Medical Investigations Office of the Chief Medical Examiner, Report of Investigation By Medical Examiner, Ashley Taylor, 5 Aug 2011.


**Chapter 9: A Day In the Life of EKG47US**

Official Transcript of Proceedings, January 28th and 29th, 2013, In the District Court of Okfuskee County, State of Oklahoma. State of Oklahoma v. Kevin Sweat. CF-11-126 and C-2014-930. Volume I, Witness Testimony of Edward Franklin Silvey, Jr. pp. 98-134

Official Transcript of Proceedings, January 28th and 29th, 2013, In the District Court of Okfuskee County, State of Oklahoma. State of Oklahoma v. Kevin Sweat. CF-11-126 and C-2014-930. Volume II, Witness Testimony of Jerry Robert Bryan. pp. 136 - 141

Official Transcript of Proceedings, January 28th and 29th, 2013, In the District Court of Okfuskee County, State of Oklahoma. State of Oklahoma v. Kevin Sweat. CF-11-126 and C-2014-930. Volume II, Witness Testimony of Smokey Patchin. pp. 142 - 159

Official Transcript of Proceedings, January 28th and 29th, 2013, In the District Court of Okfuskee County, State of Oklahoma. State of Oklahoma v. Kevin Sweat. CF-11-126 and C-2014-930. Volume II, Witness Testimony of James Kennedy. pp. 160 - 171

Official Transcript of Proceedings, January 28th and 29th, 2013, In the District Court of Okfuskee

County, State of Oklahoma. State of Oklahoma v.
Kevin Sweat. CF-11-126 and C-2014-930. Volume
II, Witness Testimony of John Woods. pp. 172- 184

Official Transcript of Proceedings, January 28th
and 29th, 2013, In the District Court of Okfuskee
County, State of Oklahoma. State of Oklahoma v.
Kevin Sweat. CF-11-126 and C-2014-930. Volume
II, Witness Testimony of Terrance Higgs. pp. 185 -
243

Hermann, Peter. "Baltimore police gun traced to
Oklahoma killings" The Baltimore Sun. 17 Dec 11.
Web:
http://www.baltimoresun.com/news/bs-md-ci-police-
gun-murder-20111215-story.htmlThe Baltimore
Sun.


**Chapter 10: The Prosecution**
"Those elements are first, the death of a human;"
from Oklahoma Uniform Jury Instructions, Criminal
2nd Edition. OUJI-CR 4-61: Murder In The First
Degree With Malice Aforethought - Elements

"Malice aforethought," from Oklahoma Uniform Jury
Instructions, Criminal 2nd Edition. OUJI-CR 4-62:
Murder in the First Degree - Definition and
Explanation of Malice Aforethought

"The State presented numerous aggravating circumstances" from Bill of Particulars In Re Punishment, State of Oklahoma vs. Kevin Joe Sweat, Case No. CF-2011-126, filed 9 Dec 11 in the District Court of the Twenty-Fourth Judicial District of the State of Oklahoma Sitting In and For Okfuskee County

"reserved for the worst of crimes and limited in its instances of application." from Evola, Matt. *American Criminal Law Review.* Georgetown Law. 10 Feb 16 citing Kennedy v. Louisiana, 554 U.S. 407, 447 (2008)

"Oklahoma is one of thirty one states left in the union to apply the death penalty." from States and Capital Punishment, National Conference of State Legislatures. 6 Jun 18. Web: www.ncls.org

"The Eighth Amendment of the Constitution limits capital punishment "to those offenders who commit a narrow category of the most serious crimes and whose extreme culpability makes them the most deserving of execution." from Evola, Matt. *American Criminal Law Review.* Georgetown Law. 10 Feb 16 citing Kennedy v. Louisiana, 554 U.S. 407, 420 (2008)

"Aggravating factors in the State of Oklahoma" from Oklahoma Uniform Jury Instructions, Criminal 2nd edition, OUJI-CR 4-72, 2017 supplement [see email for link]

"Mitigating factors include any aspect of a defendant's character" from Eddings v. Oklahoma, (1982)

"aggravating factors must outweigh the mitigating ones" from Evola, Matt. *American Criminal Law Review*. Georgetown Law. 10 Feb 16, citing People v. Young, 814 P.2d 834, 846-47 (Colo. 1991)

"Oklahoma Indigent Defense System" from https://www.ok.gov/OIDS/

"Wayne Woodyard, a seasoned defense attorney who specialized in death penalty cases" from Erwin, Mike. "Murder Case Proceeding Slowly" *Pawhuska Journal-Capital*. 29 April 13. Print.

"I knew without a doubt" from Aspinwall, Cary. "Judge Closes Portion of Hearing" *Tulsa World*. 20 Dec 13. Web: https://www.tulsaworld.com/news/courts/judge-closes-portion-of-hearing-in-case-involving-slayings-of/article_7315927a-1411-5cf0-9ac2-ff3efab19f10.html

"I see demons, vampires ... monsters, demons, whatever." from Associated Press. "Death Penalty Off Table" *The San Diego Tribune*. 4 Jul 11. Web:

http://www.sandiegouniontribune.com/sdut-death-p
enalty-off-table-for-triple-murder-suspect-2014jul04-
story.html

"review the cell phone records" from  Official
Transcript of Proceedings, January 28th and 29th,
2013, In the District Court of Okfuskee County,
State of Oklahoma. State of Oklahoma v. Kevin
Sweat. CF-11-126 and C-2014-930. Volume II,
Witness Testimony of Kenneth Titsworth. pp. 184 -
228.

"Sweat told Titsworth that he saw two monsters"
from Wofford, Jerry. "Shell Casings at Scene" Tulsa
World. 11 Dec 11. Web:
https://www.tulsaworld.com/news/crimewatch/shell-
casings-at-scene-led-police-to-weleetka-arrest/articl
e_a81972ee-bd18-5a54-8dbe-c27369c57c8a.html

"The Kevin I see in there isn't the Kevin" from
NewsOn6.com. "Man Charged In Weleetka
Murders Appears In Court." 28 Jun 13. Web:
http://www.newson6.com/story/20721418/man-char
ged-in-weleetka-girls-murder-in-court-for-hearing

Chapter 11: A System of Men
"admonished them to take a deep breath and
relax."
 "...we sometimes forget how great a country we
have." from TRANSCRIPT OF PROCEEDINGS,

State of Oklahoma v. Kevin Sweat, 28 Jan 2013, filed in district court 12 Feb 2013. Volume III of III, pp. 272

"Astor: I think you told Miss Reilly that the fire pit was about twenty-five feet from the house?" from from TRANSCRIPT OF PROCEEDINGS, State of Oklahoma v. Kevin Sweat, 28 Jan 2013, filed in district court 12 Feb 2013. Testimony of Curtis Sweat, pp. 76

"Defense attorney Woodyard started" from TRANSCRIPT OF PROCEEDINGS, State of Oklahoma v. Kevin Sweat, 28 Jan 2013, filed in district court 12 Feb 2013. Volume III of III, Kenneth Titsworth, pp. 194 - 218.

"Woodyard said, "Now, we understand that," from TRANSCRIPT OF PROCEEDINGS, State of Oklahoma v. Kevin Sweat, 28 Jan 2013, filed in district court 12 Feb 2013. Volume III of III, pp. 222.

"held for naught" from TRANSCRIPT OF PROCEEDINGS, January 28 and 29, 2013, State of Oklahoma vs. Kevin Sweat, C-2014-930, filed Feb 12, 2013, Volume II of III, pp. 95 - 130

"basically death of a human" from TRANSCRIPT OF PROCEEDINGS, January 28 and 29, 2013, State of Oklahoma vs. Kevin Sweat, C-2014-930, filed Feb 12, 2013, Volume II of III, page 221.

"cause of death and the manner of death is uncertain in this case." from Autopsy of Ashley Taylor, Office of the Chief Medical Examiner, 26 Aug 2011.

'When I got there Kevin Sweat" from Official Transcript of Proceedings, January 28th and 29th, 2013, In the District Court of Okfuskee County, State of Oklahoma. State of Oklahoma v. Kevin Sweat. CF-11-126 and C-2014-930. Volume III, Witness Testimony of Kenneth Titsworth. pp. 273 - 293

## Chapter 12: Pieces Left To Be Found
"Sweat gave contradictory answers on a battery of psychological tests that examined personality traits" "he didn't want me to know a lot about him," from Aspinwall, Cary. "Psychologist Finds No Mental Confusion in Murder Defendant Kevin Sweat" *The Tulsa World* 23 Apr 14. Web: https://www.tulsaworld.com/news/courts/competenc y-hearing-for-murder-defendant-kevin-sweat-stretch es-into-hours/article_36857622-c687-51a3-bf22-bd 3e3dda3def.html

"accumulated a lifetime of pain, humiliation and anger" from State of Oklahoma Court of Criminal Appeals, Opinion Denying Certiorari. Sweat v.

State of Oklahoma, C-2014-930. Filed 31 Aug 15. pp.23

"Dr. Gary Jones found that Kevin had "Asperger's Disorder which could explain some of his unusual behaviors. (p.25) Finally, Dr. Benjamin Frumpkin reported that Sweat had Schizotypal Personality Disorder" from State of Oklahoma Court of Criminal Appeals, Opinion Denying Certiorari. Sweat v. State of Oklahoma, C-2014-930. Filed 31 Aug 15. pp.23pp. 25

'Okay. Now would I be accurate in stating that as you listen..." from Official Transcript of Proceedings, January 28th and 29th, 2013, In the District Court of Okfuskee County, State of Oklahoma. State of Oklahoma v. Kevin Sweat. CF-11-126 and C-2014-930. Volume III, Witness Testimony of Kenneth Titsworth. pp. 273 - 293

"Woodyard went for the hail Mary" from Official Transcript of Proceedings, January 28th and 29th, 2013, In the District Court of Okfuskee County, State of Oklahoma. State of Oklahoma v. Kevin Sweat. CF-11-126 and C-2014-930. Volume III, pp. 221

"Kevin began physically and mentally abusing her' from Aspinwall, Cary. "Prosecutors: Kevin Sweat Threatened to Kill Girlfriend" 10 Jul 14. Web:

http://www.tulsaworld.com/news/courts/prosecutors
-kevin-sweat-threatened-to-kill-girlfriend-one-month
-before/article_648f54a7-6226-5a3c-a0c9-2e6a9e1
8557f.html

"He ordered the defendant to be bound over to face
trial on murder in the first degree." from
TRANSCRIPT OF PROCEEDINGS, January 28
and 29, 2013, State of Oklahoma vs. Kevin Sweat,
C-2014-930, filed Feb 12, 2013, Volume II of III,
page 226.

## Chapter 13: Judgment Day

"Kevin refused to allow it as mitigating evidence"
from Clay, Nolan. "Murderer given three life
sentences without parole in killings" The
Oklahoman. 24 Oct 14. Web:
http://newsok.com/article/5359779

"Sweat entered a blind plea of guilty" from
Aspinwall, Cary. "Sweat pleads guilty to 3 murders"
The Tulsa World. 01 Aug 14 Web:
https://www.tulsaworld.com/sweat-pleads-guilty-to-
murders/article_a2bbd002-b3b4-54c7-b4ca-6a8582
fa8075.html

"The criminologist surmised that Kevin viewed the
reporter as 'the Lone Ranger'" from Cross, Phil.
"Kevin Sweat Reaches Out From Behind Bars" Fox
25 News. 22 May 14. Web:

http://okcfox.com/archive/kevin-sweat-reaches-out-from-behind-bars

"Sweat had taken up correspondence with a reporter" from Cross, "Gruesome new details emerge in murders of 2 girls from Weleetka" *FoxNews 25*. 16 Jun 2015. Web: https://okcfox.com/archive/gruesome-new-details-emerge-is-murders-of-two-girls-from-weleetka

"Kevin ultimately claimed that the OSBI had dressed someone up to look like him during the recorded confession tapes." from Cross, Phil. "Judge denies Sweat's motion to withdraw guilty plea" *Fox25 News*. 31 Oct 14 http://okcfox.com/archive/kevin-sweat-heads-back-to-court-wants-to-withdraw-plea

"This was judgment day." from Clay, Nolan. "Murderer Kevin Sweat Given 3 Life Sentences" *The Oklahoman*. 24 Oct 14. Web: http://newsok.com/article/5359779

"I'm withdrawing my guilty plea" from Emory, Brian. "Kevin Sweat attacks lawyer with razor" *News9.com*. 24 Oct 14. Web: http://www.news9.com/story/26884158/sentencing-for-kevin-sweat-delayed-after-courthouse-incident

"it was only through zealous representation of defense counsel" from Rosbrugh, Laura. "Murderer

Kevin Joe Sweat Attempts Again to Withdraw guilty plea" *Okmulgee News Network*. 08 Sep 15. Web: http://www.okmulgeenews.net/newscast/item/3612-murderer-kevin-joe-sweat

"Mike Taylor expressed his relief" from Mummulo, Burt. "The Weleetka Murders - Long Road to Justice" *KTUL.com*. 31 Jul 14. Web: http://ktul.com/archive/the-weleetka-murders-long-road-to-justice

Noland, L. "Convicted child killer Kevin Sweat attacks attorney" *KFOR.com*. 24 Oct 14. Web: https://kfor.com/2014/10/24/convicted-child-killer-kevin-sweat-gets-life-in-prision-courtroom-drama-unfolds/

"Guards conducted a thorough search" from Bryan, Emory. "Kevin Sweat attacks lawyer with razor" *News9.com*. 24 Oct 14. Web: http://www.news9.com/story/26884158/sentencing-for-kevin-sweat-delayed-after-courthouse-incident

"The person who would have killed these girls" from Cross, Phil. "Criminal profiler says Weleetka murders may not be fully solved" *Fox25 News*. 16 Sep 14. Web: http://okcfox.com/archive/criminal-profiler-says-weleetka-murders-may-not-be-fully-solved

## Chapter 14: The Judge

"The prison was built in 1908" from State of Oklahoma Department of Corrections. Web: http://doc.ok.gov/oklahoma-state-penitentiary

"Titsworth received accolades" from Press Release, Oklahoma State Bureau of Investigation. 16 Dec 11. Web: https://www.ok.gov/osbi/Press_Room/2011_Press_Releases/PR-2011-12-16__2011_OSBI_AGENT_O F_THE_YEAR_NAMED.html

"After six years passed"
"Jumpy the Turtle"
"Material for the memorial garden"
"Now we know for sure" from Aspinwall, Cary. "Kevin Sweat's Long and Twisted Path to a Guilty Plea" *The Tulsa World*. 3 Aug 14 Web: https://www.tulsaworld.com/news/specialreports/sw eattrial/kevin-sweat-s-long-and-twisted-path-to-a-gu ilty/article_88c7967e-52cf-5676-879d-b2d7de52f21 e.html

"She took on a case that prosecuted an Oklahoma State Trooper" from Goforth, Dylan. "Former OHP Trooper Ordered To Trial In Rape Case." *The Frontier*. 5 Jun 15. Web: *https://www.readfrontier.org/stories/former-ohp-trooper -ordered-to-trial-in-rape-case/*

"The governor noted" from Press Release, Office of the Governor of the State of Oklahoma. "Governor Fallin Appoints Maxey Reilly Associate District Judge of Okfuskee County" 8 Aug 17. Web: http://www.publicnow.com/view/2D6C410E19E4C2 70E9DF40BCF9950DDC92153B26?2017-08-18-21 :00:08+01:00-xxx1899

23631920R00150

Made in the USA
Columbia, SC
13 August 2018